A Gift

George Zeir...

July 23rd 2006

{ Pastor:
  Grover Holder
  July 23rd 2006 }

God's Gift of Tongues

God's Gift of Tongues

The Nature, Purpose,
and Duration of Tongues
as Taught in the Bible

By

GEORGE W. ZELLER

Wipf & Stock
PUBLISHERS
Eugene, Oregon

Wipf and Stock Publishers
199 W 8th Ave, Suite 3
Eugene, OR 97401

God's Gift of Tongues
The Nature, Purpose, and Duration of Tongues as Taught in the Bible
By Zeller, George W.
Copyright©1978 by Zeller, George W.
ISBN: 1-59752-406-9
Publication date 10/1/2005
Previously published by Loizeaux Brothers, Inc., 1978

This book is gratefully dedicated
to my Faithful Pastor
GEORGE F. PARSONS
who has not shunned
to declare unto me
the whole counsel of God
so that I in turn
might teach others also

CONTENTS

HISTORICAL BACKDROP

The Lord Jesus Christ came to His own people (Matthew 1:21; 2:6) but the nation Israel did not receive Him as their Messiah, King, and Saviour (John 1:11). They wanted a King who could feed and heal their bodies (John 6:26), but cared not for a Saviour who could feed and heal their souls (John 6:58-66). Christ, through His miracles and mighty works, gave unmistakable and undeniable evidence that He was indeed the Messiah, the Son of the living God; yet the Jews in their unbelief still asked for a sign (John 2:18; Matthew 12:38-40; 13:58; Luke 4:23; 1 Corinthians 1:22).

Hundreds of years earlier Isaiah had predicted that the Messiah would perform such miracles (Isaiah 35:5-6; compare what Jesus said to John's disciples in Matthew 11:2-6). But even though the Jews saw His works (Matthew 12:13,22) and had clear proof that He was the Messiah (Matthew 12:23), they still refused to acknowledge who He was. In their wicked unbelief and blasphemy they dared to accuse Christ of performing His miracles by the power of Satan rather than by the Spirit of God (Matthew 12:24-37). Such rejection can only bring the judgment of God (Matthew 12:41-45).

9

The climactic rejection of the Messiah took place when the Jews said to Pilate, "Let Him be crucified" (Matthew 27:21-23). Even worse, they took full responsibility for their actions: "His blood be on us, and on our children" (Matthew 27:25). God indeed held them responsible for what they had done: "[Him] ye have taken, and by *wicked* hands have crucified and slain" (Acts 2:23).

The Lord, because of His forbearance and long-suffering, did not judge the nation immediately. In fact, God graciously made known the gospel to the *Jew first* (Romans 1:16; Acts 2:5; 3:26). They should have been the last to hear! In fact, *they did not deserve to hear at all*. But God in His matchless grace reached out to the nation which had crucified His Son!

When Paul entered a city he normally went to the synagogue first, often encountering great resistance to the gospel (Acts 13:44-50; 18:4-6; 28:23-28; cf., Romans 11:28). Yet God patiently waited and gave the nation opportunity to repent. When Paul finally appeared in Jerusalem (Acts 21–22) the Jews once again rejected God's message and God's messenger. They even tried to kill him, crying, "Away with him" (Acts 21:36; 22:22), even as they had done to the Saviour years before (John 19:15).

The day of God's long-suffering must come to an end. Years before, the Lord Jesus had predicted that a terrible judgment of God would come upon Jerusalem because of their unbelief (Matthew 23:38; 24:2; Luke 21:5-6). About forty years after the crucifixion of

Christ this prediction was literally fulfilled. In 70 A.D. the Roman General Titus captured and *completely* destroyed Jerusalem with great slaughter. Since this time the nation Israel has been without a king, without a prince, without a sacrifice, without a priesthood, and without a temple (Hosea 3:4). For nearly 2000 years the Jewish people have been scattered and persecuted throughout the world. Instead of enjoying God's blessings, they have been under God's curse (see Deuteronomy 28).

In this century a remarkable event has taken place in Jewish history. A nation has been reborn! The Hebrew language has been revived! Hundreds of Jews have been returning to their homeland. God has providentially been setting the stage for the events which must shortly come to pass. Even though many Israelites now occupy the land, they are there, for the most part, in unbelief. Though a small Christ-rejecting remnant has returned, the vast majority of Jews are still dispersed throughout the nations of the world. During the Second World War, about one third of all the Jews in the world (six million) perished under German persecution. There is coming another day in which two thirds will die (Zechariah 13:9). Certainly Israel is still under the terrible curse of God. But a brighter day is coming in which the nation Israel will be delivered, forgiven, and purified (Jeremiah 30:7-9; Romans 11:26-27). At this time the nation will begin to enjoy the millennial blessings of God (Isaiah 33:17-24).

SECTION 1

THE GIFT OF TONGUES

PREDICTED

IN THE GREAT COMMISSION

OF THE CHURCH

Mark 16

CHAPTER 1

TONGUES PREDICTED
BY CHRIST

Mark 16

Following His resurrection and prior to His return to the right hand of the Majesty on high, the Lord Jesus gave commandments to the apostles whom He had chosen (Acts 1:2). One such command is recorded in Mark 16:15: "Go ye into *all the world,* and preach the gospel *to every creature.*" Christ sent His disciples to herald the good news to every kindred and tongue and people and nation—*to every creature.*

The worldwide scope of this commission stands in marked contrast to another commission, one that our Lord gave to the very same men just a couple of years earlier:

These twelve Jesus sent forth, and commanded them, saying, Go not into the way of the Gentiles, and into any city of the Samaritans enter ye not: But go rather to the lost sheep of the house of Israel (Matthew 10:5-6).

15

Prior to the cross our Lord's ministry was confined to *a nation.* Today the gospel is proclaimed among *all nations.* Israel was once the center of God's program. Today God has Christian assemblies (local churches) scattered throughout the world. Jerusalem was the focal point during the previous dispensation. Today, Jerusalem is merely recognized as the starting point of God's new program (Luke 24:47).

The great commission revealed for the first time this significant shift from *one nation* to *every nation.* Notice the worldwide scope of the great commission:

As recorded by Matthew:
> "teach *all nations*" (28:19)

As recorded by Mark:
> "Go ye into *all the world*" (16:15)
> "Preach the gospel *to every creature*" (16:15)
> "[they] preached *everywhere*" (16:20)

As recorded by Luke:
> "repentance and remission of sins should be preached in His name *among all nations*" (24:47)

> "Ye shall be witnesses unto Me
> both in Jerusalem (the starting point—24:47)
> and in all Judea (the home of the Jews)
> and in Samaria (the home of the Samaritans)
> and unto the uttermost part of the earth (the home of the Gentiles)" (Acts 1:8)

As recorded by John:
> "[I have] sent them *into the world*" (17:18; cf. 20:21)

God's chosen people were once numbered among *a nation*. To find God's faithful remnant according to the election of grace, one would look *within* the nation Israel: "I have left me seven thousand *in Israel*, all the knees which have not bowed unto Baal" (1 Kings 19:18). Today God's chosen people are *among all nations* (cf. Luke 24:47), representing Christ throughout the world.

Who were these men who were given this worldwide commission? What were their credentials? Certainly they were not among the rulers of Israel. None of the eleven were members of the Sanhedrin. They were opposed by the Jewish religious leaders of their day. Who were these common, ordinary men? They were merely a band of "unlearned and ignorant men" (Acts 4:13), including several fishermen and a publican! They were *nobodies* telling *everybody* about *somebody* who could save *anybody*! They had a life-changing gospel which they were commanded to proclaim, not to the Jews only, but also to the Samaritans and the nations of the world.

Imagine the response of the unbelieving Jews as they witnessed the intense evangelistic activity of these early disciples. One can almost hear their objections:

"What right do you men have to preach a message of reconciliation to pagan Gentiles and mongrel Samaritans with whom we should have no dealings? How can you offer forgiveness to those outside of the commonwealth of Israel? Do you not know that God's witness on earth is the nation Israel, and that it is only through this nation that men can come to know the true and living God?

"Jerusalem is the holy city, and the Temple is where God manifests His presence. What right do you have to announce to the nations that they can get right with God *apart from circumcision* and *apart from Judaism*? Salvation is of the Jews. Why do you seek to drastically alter God's purpose and program which must have its center of operation in the chosen nation of Israel?"*

Surely our Lord was aware of these problems which would face His apostles, and He knew that these men lacked certain credentials. So not only did Christ give them a message to preach, but also He gave them a promise of *signs* which would serve to confirm and authenticate the gospel message:

> And these signs shall follow those who believe. . . .
> And they went forth, and preached everywhere, the Lord
> working with them, and *confirming the word with signs*
> following (Mark 16:17,20).

---

* It is noteworthy that in Acts 8 the Ethiopian eunuch came to Jerusalem seeking to worship, and to come to know the true and living God. Not until he left the city to return home did he hear the message of life. Jerusalem failed to give him what he had come to find.

One remarkable sign here predicted by the Lord Jesus was that the disciples would be given the ability to "speak with new tongues" (Mark 16:17). This is the first mention of the *gift* of tongues in the Bible— a promise given by the risen Lord and soon to be fulfilled on the day of Pentecost.

A CONFIRMATORY SIGN

According to Mark 16:20, the purpose of these *sign-gifts* was to *confirm* (establish, strengthen) *the word* of the apostles (compare Hebrews 2:3-4). Consider, for example, the gift of healing. When the apostles went forth preaching, they announced to men everywhere that *forgiveness of sins* could be received by faith in Christ:

Repent, and be baptized every one of you in the name of Jesus Christ for the remission [forgiveness] of sins (Acts 2:38).

Repent, therefore, and be converted, that your sins may be blotted out (Acts 3:19).

Him hath God exalted with His right hand to be a Prince and a Saviour, to give repentance to Israel, and forgiveness of sins (Acts 5:31).

To Him give all the prophets witness, that through His name whosoever believeth in Him shall receive *remission* [forgiveness] of sins (Acts 10:43).

What right did these uneducated fishermen have to offer such forgiveness to men? How could they preach with such authority? Did this message really originate from God? Should a message coming from such common and ordinary men be believed?

In Acts 3 Peter and John met a certain man who was lame from his mother's womb. Imagine Peter challenging the crowd by saying:

> Which is easier to say to this lame man, "Your sins are forgiven if you believe in Christ" or "Arise, get up and walk"?

Obviously, Peter's authority in the spiritual realm could not be visibly demonstrated. It is impossible to look within a man and see if his sins are actually forgiven. But in order to prove that his promise of forgiveness was valid, Peter performed a miracle in the physical realm which no one could deny (Acts 4:13-16). Thus Peter continues:

> But that you may know that God has power to forgive sins in the name of Christ [he says to the lame man] in the name of Jesus Christ of Nazareth rise up and walk (compare Mark 2:5-12).

Thus God confirmed the word of His apostles, bearing them witness, both with signs and wonders, and with various miracles and gifts of the Holy Spirit (Hebrews 2:4).

How then did the gift of tongues serve to confirm the word of the apostles? Perhaps this is best illustrated in the account of the conversion of Cornelius and his household (Acts 10). For the very first time the door of faith was opened to the Gentiles, a spiritual fact which the Jews found extremely difficult to believe. Would the God of Israel really accept Gentiles into His Church and give them all the spiritual benefits that saved Jews enjoyed?

Such a concept was utterly foreign to the Jewish mind! Peter (who had already heard the great commission and who was given the command to preach to *every* creature) had to be given the thrice-repeated visual object lesson of a supernatural trance before he finally got the message (Acts 10:9-18)! But Peter learned that God was able even to take an unclean Gentile and provide the needed cleansing through Christ (Acts 10:28).

Peter learned this lesson so well that his message to Cornelius and those Gentiles with him was saturated with universalism. It was a message which would have shocked contemporary Judaism! Notice Peter's emphasis:

God is no respecter of persons! Jew or Gentile— there is no difference (Acts 10:34; cf. Romans 3:22)!

God accepts people *in every nation* (Acts 10:35).

God is *Lord of all*! Is He the God of the Jews only? Is He not also of the Gentiles? Yes, of the Gentiles also (Acts 10:36; cf. Romans 3:29)!

Whoever believes in Christ (not just Jews but Gentiles also) shall receive forgiveness of sins (Acts 10:43; cf. Romans 10:12-13)!

Thus a mere fisherman announced to these Gentiles that they could enjoy God's full salvation by faith in Christ alone, apart from circumcision and apart from becoming a Jewish proselyte! Imagine the Jewish reaction to such a message:

"Peter, for hundreds of years God's full blessings could come to a Gentile only through the nation Israel, God's witness on earth. What right do you have to receive Gentiles on an equal basis with Jews? If Israel is God's chosen nation, then how can God accept people in every nation? By what authority do you promote such a strange and novel doctrine? Is this teaching really of God?"

Once again God stood behind His servant Peter, and gave an authenticating sign to prove that these Gentiles had been accepted into the Church on an equal basis, and as fellow members of the same body (Ephesians 3:6). Although no one was healed, a remarkable miracle took place. These believing Gentiles began to speak with new tongues, a miraculous manifestation identical to what the Jews had experienced on the day of Pentecost. As a result, those Jews who were present with Peter were astonished that the Gentiles had also received the gift of the Holy Spirit (Acts 10:45-46).

Thus tongues was an outward evidence that these Gentiles had been fully received into the body of

Christ by means of Spirit-baptism (Acts 11:15-17). Indeed, these Gentiles were the recipients of every spiritual blessing in Christ. When the Jews heard of the repeated manifestation of this sign-gift, they could only conclude that "God hath also to the Gentiles granted repentance unto life" (Acts 11:18). So the word of a Galilean fisherman was wonderfully confirmed by the living God.

A SUPERNATURAL GIFT

In Mark 16:17-18, the gift of tongues is classified with other gifts which were obviously supernatural. God-given power and authority is required in order to cast out demons and heal the sick (cf. Matthew 10:1). Miraculous protection is needed in order to be delivered from the effects of deadly venom and deadly poison. Tongues is here included in a list of miraculous, supernatural sign-gifts (cf. 1 Corinthians 12:9-10, 29-30). Therefore the ability to speak in a tongue was a supernatural, God-given ability (cf. Acts 2:4). Today, in contrast, "speaking in tongues" most often takes the form of "ecstatic utterances" which can readily be attained psychologically by a person who reaches a state of religious and emotional ecstasy.

FOREIGN LANGUAGES

When the Lord first mentioned the gift of tongues He described and defined the word "tongues" by the adjective "new": "they shall speak with *new* tongues" (Mark 16:17). The word "new" means "new, unknown, strange."[1] Thus tongues is the supernatural (God-given) ability whereby a person is able to speak in a tongue that he has never spoken in before, one that is totally *new* to him. We would speak in similar terms today: "I'm going to school and learn a *new* language." The language itself is not new, but it is new to the one who has never previously learned it.

The fulfillment of the Lord's prediction that new tongues would be spoken took place only fifty days after the resurrection. It was then, on the day of Pentecost, that the Spirit of God was poured out upon those Jewish believers in a unique and wonderful way, and the Church of Jesus Christ was born.

SECTION 2

THE GIFT OF TONGUES

FULFILLED

IN THE EARLY CHURCH

Acts 2; 10; 19

CHAPTER 2

TONGUES FULFILLED
AT PENTECOST

Acts 2

Pentecost marks the beginning of the Church. On this important day Spirit-baptism first took place (see Ephesians 1:22-23 and 1 Corinthians 12:13; compare with Matthew 3:11; 16:18; Acts 1:5; 11:15-17). Thus for the first time believers were immersed into a new and unique organism, the body of Christ. God's new program was inaugurated on this momentous day!

This day also marks the beginning of the gift of tongues. For the first time the Lord's promise of Mark 16:17 was fulfilled as the disciples spoke with new tongues. Tongues as a *sign-gift* made its first historical appearance in Acts 2.

We can safely conclude, then, that tongues was a *sign* which served to *signal* some aspect of God's new program. Tongues pointed to the fact that God was doing something new and different! No longer would God's witness be a nation (Isaiah 43:10-12), but God's

27

witnesses would be among all nations (Acts 1:8; Luke 24:47; cf. Colossians 1:27). No longer would Jerusalem be the focal point (cf. 1 Kings 10:1-9), rather it would be merely the starting point (Luke 24:47; Acts 1:8). No longer would God's message go only to the lost sheep of the house of Israel (Matthew 10:5-6), but it would go to every nation and kindred and people and *tongue* (Matthew 28:19-20; Revelation 5:9).

As a nation, Israel, through unbelief and rebellion, failed to be faithful custodians of the truth of God, and they even crucified the Lord of glory. As a result the nation was temporarily laid aside (Romans 9—11) and God is presently taking from the nations a people for His Name (Acts 15:14). To signal such a drastic and consequential change of program, God gave a very simple sign (object lesson) to an unbelieving nation— the gift of tongues.

Tongues, since the ancient experience of Babel, has conveyed an ominous message of rebellion, judgment, and dispersion (Genesis 11, and compare Deuteronomy 28:49; Isaiah 28:11; Jeremiah 5:15). Now, at the beginning of the church age, God sets forth this doomful and judgmental sign to a rebellious people whose official judgment at the hands of the Romans was only forty years away (70 A.D.), to be followed by a worldwide dispersion that would last for 2000 years!!

> And they were all filled with the Holy Ghost, and began to speak with other tongues, as the Spirit gave them utterance (Acts 2:4).

On the day of Pentecost the disciples spoke with "other tongues" (cf. 1 Corinthians 14:21). The adjective "other" (*heterais*) could be translated "different." They spoke in "different tongues." The word "tongues" is plural, indicating that they spoke in many languages on that day—languages which were "different" from what they had previously known or spoken. So ·the tongues that they spoke were both *new* (Mark 16:17) and *different* (Acts 2:4).

How were they able to speak in different tongues? Obviously they would need supernatural enabling to speak in new and different languages. Thus we read that "the *Spirit* gave them utterance." It was the Spirit of God who enabled them to "speak forth" in such a unique way. The gift of tongues was a supernatural, Spirit-given ability (cf. Acts 2:15-17).

> And there were dwelling at Jerusalem Jews, devout men, out of every nation under heaven (Acts 2:5).

It is highly significant that on this special day God had Jewish representatives present from "every nation under heaven." It is as if God were saying to these Jews: "I want you to understand what is involved in My *new program*, and I want you to appreciate the worldwide scope of My great commission (cf. Matthew 28:19; Mark 16:15; Luke 24:47). Therefore I am going to give you a preview of world evangelization. I am going to give you an audio-visual aid (namely, *tongues*) to show you that God's message is going to go to every nation under Heaven, even to every nation that is represented here today."

As Merril F. Unger has noted: "The supernatural display of languages at Pentecost was a harbinger of the dominant feature of worldwide evangelism to be realized in the new age and was a sign to the Jews that the Holy Spirit had been given to work out in believers Christ's glorious salvation purchased on the cross and to equip them to proclaim the wonderful message of this salvation to every creature under heaven."[2]

> Now when this was noised abroad, the multitude came together, and were confounded, because that every man heard them speak in his own language (Acts 2:6).

The multitude caught wind that something strange and extraordinary was taking place, so they assembled together to investigate this phenomenon. Why were they confounded and perplexed? Because every one of these Jews (who were from every nation under Heaven) heard them speak in his own language or dialect (*dialektōi*, the language of a particular nation or region). It is obvious then that the different tongues which they heard were real languages.

> And they were all amazed and marvelled, saying one to another, Behold, are not all these which speak Galileans? And how hear we every man in our own tongue, wherein we were born? (Acts 2:7-8)

These Jews were amazed because of the miracle of Galileans speaking in foreign languages (compare Mark 14:70). "How can Galileans be speaking in our native tongue?" The word translated "tongue" is again the word "language." The Galilean disciples were speaking in the *native languages* of these Jews who had come from all over the known world.

At the time of the King James translation (1611), the word "tongues" simply meant "languages."* This can be seen in the translation of Revelation 9:11. The text simply gives a name "in Hebrew" and "in Greek" (see NASV) but the translators of the KJV say, "in the Hebrew tongue" and "in the Greek tongue." The word "tongue," which is not in the Greek text, is obviously inserted as a synonym for "language."[3]

> Parthians, and Medes, and Elamites, and the dwellers in Mesopotamia, and in Judea, and Cappadocia, in Pontus, and Asia, Phrygia, and Pamphylia, in Egypt, and in the parts of Libya about Cyrene, and strangers of Rome, Jews and proselytes (Acts 2:9-10).

God's new program was for the gospel to go to all of these regions. God's message must be proclaimed to every nation and tongue under Heaven. Even on this

---

* Most editions of the Authorized King James Version contain these words on the title page: "The Holy Bible containing the Old and New Testaments translated out of the *original tongues.*" Today it would be more natural to say, "translated out of the *original languages.*"

day when the Church was born, God's message was made known to representatives of every nation under Heaven, as if God were giving the Jews a preliminary indication of His worldwide intent.

Robert G. Gramacki comments on these verses: "Not only did the disciples speak different languages, but they also spoke various dialects of the same language. The Phrygians and Pamphylians, for instance, both spoke Greek, but in different idioms; the Parthians, Medes, and Elamites all spoke Persian, but in different provincial forms."[4]

> Cretes and Arabians, we do hear them speak in our tongues the wonderful works of God (Acts 2:11).

When this verse is compared with verse 8 it becomes evident that tongues is equated with languages:

Verse 8—"We hear. . . in our own language [dialect] "
Verse 11—"We hear. . . in our tongues"

Verse 11 explains the *content* of the tongues-speaking. What did these Jews hear? Did they hear nonsense syllables? Did they hear ecstatic utterances? Did they hear unintelligible gibberish? No, they heard "the wonderful works of God," or as it could be rendered, "the great things (*megaleia*) of God." These Galileans were filled with praise for what God had done, and the Spirit gave them the ability (verse 4) to communicate this praise in languages which were foreign and unknown to them. No interpreter was needed since every man heard the message in his own native dialect (verses 8,11).

The tongues-speaking served only an indirect evangelistic purpose, in that the tongues phenomenon prepared the way for Peter's convicting message. Tongues did in Acts 2 what the healing of the lame man did in Acts 3. It served as an attention getter for the gospel message that was to follow. Tongues in Acts 2 was a *sign*, indicating and pointing to the fact that the gospel would go into all the world—to every kindred and *tongue* and people and nation (Revelation 5:9), according to the great commission of our Lord. If the gift of tongues served to signal the inauguration of God's new program, then by implication God's old program (Israel) must be set aside. The bringing in of the new necessitates the going out of the old!

> And they were all amazed, and were in doubt, saying one to another, What meaneth this? Others mocking said, These men are full of new wine (Acts 2:12-13).

It is of interest to note the reaction of these foreign Jews to the miraculous tongues-speaking (verse 12). They were all amazed and perplexed (cf. verses 7-8), and they wanted an explanation. They wanted to know the *meaning* ("What meaneth this?") of the remarkable exhibition of *different languages* which they had just witnessed. They had heard the "great things of God" communicated in their own native languages by mere Galileans! How was this possible?

"Others mocking" (verse 13) offered an explanation of the tongues spectacle. Who were these mockers? The word "others" (*heteros*) refers to a group of Jews *different* from the foreign Jews mentioned in verses 5-12. These mockers were local Jews from Palestine and Judea who apparently did not understand the foreign tongues being spoken. The tongues-speakers seemed to be producing "uncertain sounds" (1 Corinthians 14:23)!

They thus accused the Galileans of drunkenness. These mockers provided a naturalistic explanation of a phenomenon that was obviously supernatural, thus robbing the Spirit of God of the credit and honor that was due Him (cf. verse 4). Peter then seized this opportunity to address the multitude and to show the absurdity of such a naturalistic explanation.

> But Peter, standing up with the eleven, lifted up his voice, and said unto them, Ye men of Judea, and all ye that dwell at Jerusalem, be this known unto you, and hearken to my words: For these are not drunken, as ye suppose, seeing it is but the third hour of the day. But this is that which was spoken by the prophet Joel; And it shall come to pass in the last days, saith God, I will pour out of My Spirit upon all flesh: and your sons and your daughters shall prophesy, and your young men shall see visions, and your old men shall dream dreams: And on My servants and on My handmaidens I will pour out in those days of My Spirit; and they shall prophesy (Acts 2:14-18).

The first reason for the absurdity of the charge of drunkenness was the simple fact that it was only about 9:00 A.M. and people do not generally get drunk at such an hour (verse 15). (Usually that is the time when they are recovering from the night before.)

Peter's second reason is taken from Joel's prophecy concerning the supernatural outpouring of the Spirit in the last days. He used this Scripture to show that what had just taken place was obviously the miraculous working of the Spirit of God (cf. verse 4). In essence, Peter was saying to these mockers, "We are not drunk with wine, as you suppose, but we are filled with the Spirit (verse 4). Just as there will be a supernatural outpouring of the Spirit in the last days producing great signs and wonders (verses 17-20), so there has been a supernatural outpouring of the Spirit today producing the sign-gift of tongues. What you have witnessed is just what Joel spoke of—the miraculous working of the Holy Spirit! Therefore, I totally reject your absurd and naturalistic explanation of drunkenness!"

Following this sermon introduction, Peter preached unto them Christ crucified and risen. Three thousand persons responded in the right way to his message and were added to the newly-formed body of Christ, God's unique organism.

CHAPTER 3

TONGUES FULFILLED
AT CAESAREA

Acts 10

The Church, God's called-out assembly, had its beginning at Pentecost (Acts 2). For the first time believers were immersed into a living organism, the body of Christ (1 Corinthians 12:13; Acts 1:5; Acts 11:15-16). Tongues at Pentecost indicated that God was doing something new and unique.

God's purpose and program shifted from a *nation* (Israel) to *nations* (from which He would take out a people for His name—Acts 15:14), and from a *tongue* (Hebrew—the language of the Jews and the language of the Old Testament) to *tongues* (the tongues of every nation under Heaven—Acts 2:5,9-11). God's witness would no longer be *a nation* (Isaiah 43:10,12; 44:8), but God's witnesses would be *among all nations and peoples and tongues* (Acts 1:8).

Another momentous day in the history of the Church is described in Acts 8. For the first time the door of faith was opened to the people of Samaria (a mixed race—half Jew and half Gentile). They also received the Spirit and became full-fledged members of the body of Christ (Acts 8:14-17). God's new program, as outlined in Acts 1:8, was being wondrously outworked in history.

Although not specifically stated it is almost certain that the Samaritan believers also spoke in tongues when they received the gift of the Spirit. Probably it was this manifestation of tongues that so impressed Simon (Acts 8:18-19). God once again used tongues to *signal* an important turning point in the forward progress of the gospel. The Jews could not help but be impressed by this drastic change in God's dealing with men (compare Matthew 10:5; John 4:9; 8:48). The hated Samaritans were now fellow members of the same body! The enmity had been abolished at the cross (cf. Ephesians 2:13-22)!

The next great milestone in church history occurred in Acts 10. For the first time Gentiles were united into the body of Christ, having received the gift of the Spirit *just as* the Jews did in Acts 2 (see Acts 10:45-47; 11:15-17). The Gentiles became fellow members of the same body (Ephesians 3:6), joined together under the glorious Headship of Christ. Again the gift of tongues would be expected to mark this crucial phase in God's new program, as the door of faith was opened to the *nations* (Acts 14:27—the word "Gentiles" (*ethnesin*) is the word for "nations"). It was beginning to become evident that God was moving from *a nation* to *the na-*

tions!! Israel must decrease; the Gentiles must increase (Romans 11:12)!!

> While Peter yet spake these words, the Holy Ghost fell on all them which heard the word (Acts 10:44).

The Holy Spirit fell on Cornelius and his household. According to Acts 11:15-17, this means that these Gentiles were immersed (baptized) into the body of Christ. For the first time the Church had Gentile membership.

When the Church first began on the day of Pentecost its membership was entirely Jewish. Today the Church is *almost* totally composed of Gentile members (thank God for the Jewish exceptions!). The book of Acts tells how this amazing ethnic shift took place.

> And they of the circumcision which believed were astonished, as many as came with Peter, because that on the Gentiles also was poured out the gift of the Holy Ghost (Acts 10:45).

Jewish believers were present to witness what God was doing. They were amazed that the same gift which the Jews received at Pentecost was now given to these Gentiles. How did these Jews know that these Gentiles received the Spirit? Verse 46 gives the explanation.

> For they heard them speak with tongues, and magnify God (Acts 10:46).

They knew the same gift was given because it was accompanied by the *same sign*—namely, tongues. The gift of tongues was the outward evidence that these Gentiles had been the recipients of God's full salvation, which included membership in God's unique program, the Church. So it is evident that the tongues in Acts 10 were just like the tongues in Acts 2.

As they were speaking in tongues they were magnifying God. The word translated "magnifying" (*megalunontōn*) is similar to the expression found in Acts 2:11: "the wonderful works of God" (*megaleia*). With their tongues they were making God *great* (Acts 10:46) by speaking forth the *great things of God* (Acts 2:11). So every indication is that the content of the tongues-speaking was the same both in Acts 2 and in Acts 10. In both places they were praising God for His greatness and magnifying Him.

> Then answered Peter, Can any man forbid water, that these should not be baptized, which have received the Holy Ghost as well as we? (Acts 10:46-47)

Again and again it is affirmed that what happened here at Caesarea is the *very same thing* that happened on the day of Pentecost at Jerusalem. Note carefully the emphasis:

Acts 10:45—"on the Gentiles *also*"
Acts 10:47—"who have received the Holy Spirit *as well as we*"

Acts 11:1—"the Gentiles *also* [in addition to us]"

Acts 11:15—"the Holy Spirit fell on them, *as on us at the beginning*"

Acts 11:17—"God gave the *like [same] gift as He did unto us*"

Acts 11:18—"God *also* to the Gentiles"

The Jews could no longer claim spiritual superiority over the Gentiles. From this point forward they could only claim spiritual equality (Ephesians 3:6)! In the body of Christ there is neither Jew nor Gentile (Colossians 3:11).

SUMMARY

In Acts 10 Gentiles spoke with tongues and saved Jews were present as witnesses. To these Jews the gift of tongues served as an outward evidence that the Gentiles had been Spirit-baptized into the body of Christ just as the Jews were in Acts 2. Thus, tongues served to indicate that the Gentiles had become members of God's called-out assembly (the Church) and that God's program was reaching out unto the nations. Tongues served no evangelistic purpose in Acts 10. The evangelism was already done by Peter *prior* to the tongues-speaking.

Since tongues in Acts 10 was considered by these Jews as a repeat performance of Acts 2, the following conclusions about the nature of tongues in Acts 10 can be made:

Tongues in Acts 10 involved speaking in foreign languages—languages that were "unknown" and "new" to the speaker. See Acts 2:6,8.

Tongues in Acts 10 was a supernatural sign-gift, and thus the Gentiles could speak in tongues only as the Spirit enabled them and gave them utterance. See Acts 2:4.

Tongues in Acts 10 was not unintelligible gibberish, but it involved praising God and magnifying Him for His greatness by speaking forth the wonderful works of God (Acts 10:46). See Acts 2:11.

CHAPTER 4

TONGUES FULFILLED
AT EPHESUS

Acts 19

In Ephesus, the Apostle Paul found a group of about twelve Jewish disciples who were totally ignorant of God's new program. They were in the dark concerning the things that God was presently doing in the world. They were unaware of the dispensational change that had taken place following the cross. In fact, they knew nothing of the cross or the empty tomb! They were looking for the One who should come (verse 4), but they were ignorant that He had already come!

They also had no understanding concerning the unique and special ministry of the Spirit of God in this age (verse 2). Their hearts were right, but they lacked essential information. They were familiar with John's ministry, that great prophet who called *a nation* to repentance (verse 4; cf. Matthew 3:2,8) but they did not know that God's new program was to call *nations* to repentance (see Luke 24:47; Acts 17:30).

Consider the question asked in verse 2: "Have you received the Holy Spirit?" The same emphasis was found in Acts 10:44-47. In light of Paul's later teaching in the Epistles (1 Corinthians 12:13, etc.) the question could be restated: "Have you become members of God's unique organism, the Church? Have you been immersed into the body of Christ as a result of Spirit baptism?" The answer was negative and it became obvious that a rebaptism would be necessary. John's baptism of repentance for *a nation* was not sufficient. They needed the baptism which was identified with God's new program of making *Christian* disciples of *all nations* (Matthew 28:19).

Again, here in Acts 19, the emphasis is upon God's new program, the Church, whereby Israel must decrease and the nations (Gentiles) must increase (Romans 11:12). God's choice is no longer a nation, but God's choice is from among all nations (Acts 15:14), so that the living God might have a showcase of His grace (Ephesians 2:7) which He has redeemed by His blood "out of every kindred, and tongue, and people, and nation" (Revelation 5:9—the raptured Church). So tongues again serve to *signal* God's movement from one nation and one tongue to all nations and all tongues.

Very little is said about tongues-speaking in Acts 19. Verse 6 states that the gift of the Spirit was accompanied by the sign-gift of tongues (cf. Acts 10:46). *Prophecy* (the speaking forth of the Word of God—1 Corinthians 14:3) is also mentioned in connection with tongues (verse 6). Again, tongues served no evangelistic purpose. Every indication is that tongues in Acts 19 was essentially the same as tongues in Acts 2 and Acts 10.

SECTION 3

THE GIFT OF TONGUES

ABUSED

IN THE CORINTHIAN CHURCH

1 Corinthians 12–14

THE LOCAL ASSEMBLY DISPLAYING
THE LIVING GOD

The Heavenly Head is *unseen* (John 16:10; 1 Peter 1:8)
  —the Lord Jesus Christ
  (Ephesians 1:22-23; 5:23; Colossians 1:18)

The Body, the Church, is *seen* on Earth (cf. 1 Corinthians 4:9)
  —God's Called-out Assembly of Believers
  (Ephesians 4:11-16; 1 Corinthians 12:12-27)

> Its People: Lost sinners who have come to the cross
> (John 3:16; Acts 16:30-31), and thus have
> been baptized (placed) into the body
> (1 Corinthians 12:13)

> Its Purpose: To manifest, magnify and mirror its Heavenly
> Head (1 Peter 2:9; Philippians 1:20-21)

> Its Power: Healthy believers, growing and glowing, func-
> tioning together to outwork God's Word,
> and thus displaying before men and angels

> > GOD'S LIFE (Colossians 1:27; Galatians 2:20; 4:19;
> > 5:22-23; Romans 6:4)
> > GOD'S WISDOM (Ephesians 3:9-10;
> > Colossians 1:9; 2:3)
> > GOD'S POWER (Ephesians 3:20; Philippians 4:13)
> > GOD'S GRACE (Ephesians 2:7)
> > GOD'S TRUTH (1 Timothy 3:15;
> > Philippians 2:15-16; Colossians 3:16)
> > GOD'S LOVE (John 17:22-26)
> > GOD'S GLORY (Ephesians 1:6,12,14; 3:21;
> > Philippians 1:11)

CHAPTER 5

THE GIFT OF TONGUES
IN THE ASSEMBLY

1 Corinthians 12

Paul presents church truth in 1 Corinthians 12 in a most helpful and practical way. The assembly is said to be the body of Christ, with each member functioning according to the working of a sovereign God. It is imperative that this body maintain a state of health. When each believer is edified, the body will be healthy. (Compare Colossians 1:28, which emphasizes that "every" member must be healthy!) When the body is healthy, the life of Christ will be manifested, and God will be glorified as He displays Himself in and by means of the local assembly.

In making provision for the health and proper functioning of the body, God has gifted each and every believer according to His sovereign choice and will (1 Corinthians 12:7,11). First Corinthians 12:8-10 gives a list of gifts classified into three categories. This deliberate grouping into three classes is not obvious in the English text, but it is explicit in the Greek. The word translated "another" in verses 8-10 is most often the word *allos*, but the word *heteros* is used twice (in verses 9 and 10). *Heteros* is used in these verses to introduce a new and *different* class or grouping. *Allos* merely gives subdivisions of the *same* class. The gifts are classified in this way:

1 Corinthians 12:8-10

Category 1

Verse 8

to one	the word of wisdom
to another (*allos*)	the word of knowledge

Category 2

Verses 9-10

to another (*heteros*)	faith
to another (*allos*)	gifts of healing
to another (*allos*)	working of miracles
to another (*allos*)	prophecy
to another (*allos*)	discerning of spirits

Category 3

Verse 10

to another (*heteros*)	kinds of tongues
to another (*allos*)	interpretation of tongues

Tongues are listed in this third category of gifts. Thus the gift of tongues is grouped together with the gift of interpretation. The two go together. The one gift demands the other. Where there are tongues there must also be the interpretation of tongues (cf. 1 Corinthians 14:13, 27-28).

Consider first the gift of tongues. Verse 10 lists this gift and uses the expression "kinds of tongues" (*genē glōssōn*). This same expression is used in verse 28, "*diversities* [kinds] of tongues." The word "kinds" means "classes" and this indicates that tongues are *classified* into different kinds. Any linguist knows that there are many classes or kinds of languages. In fact, 1 Corinthians 14:10 makes mention of this very fact: "There are, it may be, so many *kinds* [*genē*] of voices in the world."

On the day of Pentecost it was evident that there were various *kinds of tongues* being spoken (Acts 2:7-11). Just as there are different *kinds* of reptiles (turtles, snakes, lizards, crocodiles, etc.) and yet they are all reptiles, so there are different *kinds* of tongues (Hebrew, Greek, Latin, German, etc.) and yet they are all languages.

The complementary gift listed in verse 10 is "the interpretation of tongues" (*hermēneia glōssōn*). The word translated "interpretation" is the Greek word from which comes the English word "hermeneutics," the art and science of *interpreting* the Scriptures (explaining, giving the sense, giving the meaning). When someone in the assembly spoke in a tongue, the immedi-

ate response would be something like this, "What does
it mean? Please explain. I do not understand!" In other
words, *interpretation necessitates meaning!*

Meaningless utterances cannot be interpreted.
One cannot give the meaning of something that has no
meaning. The Scriptures *can* be interpreted because
the words and sentences mean something! It is impossible to give sense to "nonsense syllables." As an example, consider these two well-known Christmas carols:

> "Gloria in Excelsis Deo"
>> ("Angels We Have Heard on High")
> "FA LA LA LA LA, LA LA LA LA"
>> ("Deck the Halls")

The first of these can be *interpreted.* It means,
"Glory to God in the highest!" The second cannot be
interpreted. It is meaningless. It is merely the emotional
expression of a person who is *jolly.*

So then, the fact that tongues necessitate interpretation indicates that tongues were not something meaningless. It was the job of the interpreter to *give the
meaning.*

Related to this noun is a verb (*hermēneuō*) which
means "to interpret." It is often used in the sense of
translation from one language to another (see John
1:38,42; 9:7; Hebrews 7:2).

Another listing of gifts is found in 1 Corinthians
12:28-29. Here the gifts are listed according to their
edificational priority (some gifts edify the assembly
more than others):

First—Apostles)
Second—Prophets) *Foundational Gifts*—Ephesians 2:20
Third—Teachers)

Last on the list—"*kinds of tongues*"

In 1 Corinthians 12:29-30 a series of questions is asked, and Paul, in a helpful way, answers his own questions. The Greek construction *demands* a negative answer to each of these questions. Are all apostles? The answer implied in the text is "*No [me]!*" Only a few specially chosen men were gifted and sent forth as apostles. Are all prophets? *No!* Only some were gifted as prophets. Are all teachers? *No!* Are all workers of miracles? *No!* Have all the gifts of healing? *No!* Do all speak with tongues? *No!*

Not every believer was gifted with the God-given ability to speak with tongues. Some, *not all*, had this gift! Do all interpret? *No!* This word "interpret" is a strengthened form of the word which was discussed in verse 10. Here in verse 30 is the word "hermeneutic" with a prefixed preposition (*dia*) which serves to strengthen the verb. Thus the word *diermēneuō* means "to interpret fully, to thoroughly give the meaning of what is said." Thayer gives for one of the meanings of this verb, "to translate into one's native language."[5] Such a usage is found in Acts 9:36 (NASV): "there was a certain disciple named Tabitha (which translated in

Greek is called Dorcas)."

"To interpret" means "to give the meaning of what is said." When something is said in a foreign language, then the *interpretation* takes the form of a translation, because in order to give the meaning of a foreign language, one must translate. Thus when a foreign missionary who knows no English comes to a church to speak, he must be accompanied by an *interpreter*, and this interpreter actually functions as a *translator*.

CHAPTER 6

THE PROBLEM OF TONGUES IN THE ASSEMBLY

1 Corinthians 13:1-3

In the first three verses of this "love" chapter, Paul sets forth a principle crucial to a correct understanding of the problem of tongues in Corinth. The principle is this: *It is possible to exercise a spiritual gift apart from love.* If it were possible, one could even speak in angelic tongues apart from love (verse 1). One may have the gifts of prophecy, knowledge, and faith, and yet not have love (verse 2). One could even suffer and die as a martyr apart from love (verse 3). In other words, a person may have a *genuine gift from God,* and yet fail to exercise that gift in love.

Such *love* can be produced in the believer only by God the Holy Spirit (Galatians 5:22) as he maintains a right relationship to the Lord (cf. Galatians 5:16; Ephesians 4:30; 1 Thessalonians 5:19). This was precisely the problem of the Corinthians. They were not walking according to love. They were walking according to the flesh: "Are ye not *carnal* [fleshly], and walk as men?" (1 Corinthians 3:1-4)

The key question is this: Does a person need to be in right relationship to the Lord in order to exercise a *genuine* spiritual gift? Consider Judas Iscariot, the son of perdition. There is no doubt that Judas was genuinely gifted of God and enabled to perform miraculous sign-gifts. According to Matthew 10:1-8, Judas actually had a part in healing the sick, cleansing the lepers, raising the dead, and casting out demons (verse 8). He even went about preaching the gospel of the kingdom (verse 7). But Judas was an *unclean, unregenerate, unsaved man* (John 13:10-11). Certainly he was not in right relationship with the Lord. Judas exercised these gifts apart from love.

The gift of tongues at Corinth was obviously being abused and misused. It was being exercised apart from love. *Love edifies* (1 Corinthians 8:1), but the tongues-speaking at Corinth did not edify (1 Corinthians 14). The misuse of the gift was causing great disorder and confusion in the assembly. But *the problem was not with the gift itself.* The gift of tongues was a *genuine* charismatic gift. Paul never implied that the gift was spurious or illegitimate. Paul never questioned the fact that the Corinthian believers actually had the God-given, miraculous ability to speak in tongues. *The real problem was with the Corinthians!* They were *misusing* the gift that God had given them and they were not exercising it in love.

God cannot be blamed for the Corinthian problem.

Tongues was a miraculous gift and God must enable a person to speak in tongues (Acts 2:4). Does this mean that when the gift was misused, *God* was misusing *His* gift? God forbid! Perish the thought! "God is not the author of confusion" (1 Corinthians 14:33). On the contrary, the *Corinthians* were misusing *His* gift. They were to blame, not God.

To solve this apparent dilemma, consider another miraculous charismatic gift, the gift of prophecy. It was possible for the gift of prophecy to be abused, and therefore Paul had to set forth some regulations in 1 Corinthians 14:29-31. Was it God's fault that His gift of prophecy was being abused? The answer is found in 1 Corinthians 14:32: "The spirits of the prophets are subject to the prophets." Dr. James L. Boyer explains this verse as follows: "The one who exercised the gift of prophecy, and also by implication the gift of tongues, was not overwhelmed by a compulsive external power which moved him automatically without his control. Rather, he was able to speak, or to wait his turn, or to refrain from speaking. In accordance with the regulations here stated, he knew what he was doing and was responsible for his actions."[6]

The gifted man was *responsible* for how he used the gift! *The problem was not with God! The problem was not with the gift! The problem was with the Corinthians!*

CHAPTER 7

THE DURATION OF TONGUES
IN THE ASSEMBLY

1 Corinthians 13:8

In 1 Corinthians 13:8 Paul makes this important statement: "Whether there be tongues, they shall *cease* [*stop*]." Tongues will cease! Paul thus predicted that this gift would stop and become inoperative. The big question which must be answered is *when*? *When* will tongues cease?

It would have been helpful had Paul been more specific: "Tongues shall cease one hundred years from now!" or "Tongues shall cease in 2000 A.D." The apostle, however, gave no such date. Obviously, at the time when Paul wrote to the Corinthians (approximately 55 A.D.), tongues had *not yet* ceased. At that time, God was still giving this gift (1 Corinthians 12:10).

When would tongues cease? *When* would the gift of tongues no longer be operative? *When* would God stop giving this gift?

Three approaches can be used in solving this

problem: the contextual approach, the historical approach, and the purposive approach. These will be briefly considered.

THE CONTEXTUAL APPROACH

Many students of the Scriptures have tried to answer the *when* question by studying 1 Corinthians 13:8 in light of the following context (verses 9-13). The key problem has been the identification of "that which is perfect" in verse 10. Since this is not the approach followed in this study, the reader is referred to helpful material found in Thomas[7] and Dillow.[8]

THE HISTORICAL APPROACH

There is overwhelming evidence that tongues did in fact *cease* early in the history of the Church. No mention of tongues can be found in any of Paul's later Epistles. The testimony of the orthodox Church Fathers lends strong support to the fact that the gift of tongues ceased. As Richard Quebedeaux has observed: "Evidence for the appearance of glossolalia, at least from the late second century to the eighteenth or nineteenth century, is scarce and frequently obscure. . . . Origen, in the third century, and Chrysostom, in the fourth, both disparaged the accounts of speaking in tongues, and rejected its continued validity. Augustine, early in the fifth century, asserted that glossolalia was a sign adapted only to biblical times."[9]

The comment by the great preacher Chrysostom is worthy of note: "This whole place is very obscure [commenting on the references to tongues in 1 Corinthians] but the obscurity is produced by our ignorance of the facts referred to and by their cessation, being such as then used to occur, but now no longer take place" (*Homilies*, XXIX, 1).[10]

For further historical documentation along these lines, see Smith,[11] Sellers,[12] Whitcomb,[13] and Dillow.[14]

THE PURPOSIVE APPROACH

What was the purpose of the gift of tongues? If the purpose for tongues is known, then it is possible to determine *when* tongues ceased. The purposive argument may be thus stated: *Tongues ceased when they no longer served the purpose for which they were given.*

This same purposive approach is helpful in considering other temporary gifts. For example, God no longer gives the gift of *apostleship* because, according to Ephesians 2:20, the apostles were foundational men. Since a solid foundation was already laid in the first century, apostles are no longer needed. They have served their purpose. When Christ began to build His Church (Matthew 16:18), He first laid the foundation and then proceeded to erect the superstructure. Today He is working on the "steeple stage," as the Church waits expectantly for His return!

Likewise, the gift of *prophecy* is no longer given

today. Prophets were necessary in the days when the New Testament was incomplete. The Church now possesses a completed Bible, and prophets are no longer needed. They have served their important purpose.

What the Church needs today is a new confrontation with the all-sufficient written Word of God (the sixty-six canonized books). Though apostles have passed off the scene, the doctrine (teaching) of the apostles remains (cf. Acts 2:42; 2 Thessalonians 2:15). Though God has ceased gifting men as prophets, there remains the God-inspired message of the prophets, namely, the completed New Testament Scriptures (2 Timothy 3:16-17; 2 Peter 1:19).

Paul used a purposive illustration in 1 Corinthians 13:11:

> When I was a child, I spoke as a child, I understood as a child, I thought as a child; but when I became a man, I put away childish things.

When a person reaches manhood, for instance, he no longer needs a baby bottle. Childish things have served their purpose and are no longer needed.

What about tongues? Has the gift of tongues served its purpose? Is this gift still needed today? What is the purpose of tongues?

These important questions will be answered in detail in Chapter 9, "The Purpose of Tongues in the Assembly." It will then be demonstrated that the gift of tongues served its God-given purpose in the early days of the Church and then *ceased no later than 70 A.D.*

CHAPTER 8

THE VALUE OF TONGUES
IN THE ASSEMBLY

1 Corinthians 14:1-20

Follow after charity ·[love], and desire spiritual
gifts, but rather that ye may prophesy (1 Corinthian 14:1).

Continuing his movement of thought from the
previous chapter, Paul sets forth a command: "Follow
after [run after, pursue, chase, as a hunter would chase
after prey or as a runner would run to the finish line to
receive a prize] love." The reason is obvious: "Love
edifies [builds up]" (1 Corinthians 8:1). Love seeks
to please his neighbor for his good to edification (Romans 15:2). Love seeks the highest and best for the
person loved. And God seeks the highest and best for
His assembly. Indeed the highest and best gift is that
of prophecy (forthtelling and communicating God's
truth to God's people). Prophecy excels in edificational
value!

65

> For he that speaketh in an unknown tongue speaketh not unto men, but unto God: for no man understandeth him; howbeit in the spirit he speaketh mysteries (1 Corinthians 14:2).

The word "unknown" was added by the translators of the King James Version. The problem in the Corinthian assembly is that the tongue which is spoken is unknown to all who are present (just as the Russian tongue would be an unknown tongue to most Americans). The person speaking in a *tongue* (unknown foreign language) does not speak to men (because no one understands what is being said) but he speaks to God (because God understands all languages). No one *understands* (literally "hears"; see Deuteronomy 28:49 in the Septuagint) the tongues-speaker! He is speaking mysteries.

The term "mystery" in the New Testament refers to truth that was once concealed and hidden and unrevealed—truth that was not previously made known (see Ephesians 3:4-5,9; Colossians 1:26; Romans 16:25). This is in contrast to verse 6 where Paul discusses truth that is revealed and made known and communicated. Truth conveyed by tongues remains mysterious *until* it is interpreted (made known, revealed, and thus understood).

> But he that prophesieth speaketh unto men to edification, and exhortation, and comfort (1 Corinthians 14:3).

The New Testament gift of prophecy is here defined by Paul. Prophecy involves God's message going forth in a clear and understandable way with the result that the saints are edified, exhorted, and comforted. This is what produces a healthy body of believers.

> He that speaketh in an unknown tongue edifieth himself; but he that prophesieth edifieth the church (1 Corinthians 14:4).

Paul now explains why the tongues-speaking at Corinth was so problematic. Tongues did not edify the Church. The tongues-speaker may edify himself, but certainly no one else. But the entire assembly could *profit* from *prophecy.*

> I would that ye all spake with tongues, but rather that ye prophesied: for greater is he that prophesieth than he that speaketh with tongues, except he interpret, that the church may receive edifying (1 Corinthians 14:5).

Paul desired that all of the Corinthians might participate in the experience of speaking in tongues (although he knew that not all believers were so gifted— 12:29-30), but much more he desired that they might exercise and enjoy the gift of prophecy. Paul did not forbid tongues, but he showed the Corinthians that prophecy was far superior to tongues on the edificational priority list. Prophecy is greater than tongues *unless* tongues are interpreted. If tongues are interpreted, then they are of the same edificational value as prophecy. In other words, tongues are edifying to the Church *if* they are interpreted. Tongues, therefore, must have edificational content! But the doctrinal riches of tongues are unlocked only by interpretation, and only then can the Church be edified.

Prophecy   = God's message understood (*edifiying*)

Tongues   = God's message not understood (*non-* without interpretation   *edifying*)

Tongues   = God's message understood (*edifying*) with interpretation

The KJV translation "except *he* interpret" is probably misleading. The verb is in the third person singular, and there are two possible ways of translating it:

    1. unless *he* [the tongues-speaker] interpret (see KJV, RV, NASV).

This implies that the tongues-speaker would be his own interpreter. It was perhaps possible that the same person could have both the gift of tongues and the gift of interpretation, but this was not necessarily the case.

    2. unless *one* [someone other than the tongues-speaker] interpret (see RSV).

This is more likely, especially in view of verses 27-28. Verse 13 may also be translated, "that *one* may interpret."

> Now, brethren, if I come unto you speaking with tongues, what shall I profit you, except I shall speak to you either by revelation, or by knowledge, or by prophesying, or by doctrine? (1 Corinthians 14:6)

What profit is tongues, *unless* tongues are converted by interpretation into these four methods of communicating the mind and will of God:

> *Revelation*—revealing and unfolding God's precious truth.
>
> *Knowledge*—making known the unsearchable riches of Christ.
>
> *Prophecy*—telling forth God's life-changing message.
>
> *Doctrine*—teaching God's holy Word of truth.

> And even things without life giving sound, whether pipe or harp, except they give a distinction in the sounds, how shall it be known what is piped or harped? (1 Corinthians 14:7)

Paul now gives two illustrations to show that *communication* is impossible apart from the recognition of *known sounds*.

Musical instruments, such as the pipe or harp (lyre), must make a recognizable *distinction* (difference) in the notes that are played. It is very easy to make nonsense sounds on a musical instrument (even a cat walking across a piano can make plenty of sounds). But to play a tune that others can recognize takes some skill and effort. One cannot play just anything. There are distinct sounds that must be played in order to produce music that sounds good and is appreciated.

This is similar to the way a foreign tongue sounds. Nothing seems to make sense. Nothing seems to go together. The ear strains for sounds that are recognizable. It *seems* and *sounds* like nonsense!

> For if the trumpet give an uncertain sound, who shall prepare himself to the battle? (1 Corinthians 14:8)

Here is Paul's second illustration—the language of trumpets. If the trumpet makes an *uncertain* (unclear, indistinct, vague) sound, then the soldier will not know whether he should charge or retreat. He will hear an unfamiliar sound coming from the trumpet and he will say, "What does that mean? I have never heard that before. Please interpret!"

> So likewise ye, except ye utter by the tongue words easy to be understood, how shall it be known what is spoken? for ye shall speak into the air (1 Corinthians 14:9).

With these illustrations in mind Paul applies the principle to the Corinthians. You must utter *words* that are *easy to be understood* (intelligible, clear, easily recognizable). This implies that tongues were *words* (not nonsense syllables) that were *not* easy to be understood. Words conveyed in a foreign tongue are not recognizable. "How can it be known what is spoken?" This implies that the gift of tongues was something that was spoken and something which had significance, but its significance could not be known *unless* the words were given in recognizable speech. If you fail to speak understandable words, then it is like speaking into the air. Your words are of no value. And the Church is not edified.

> There are, it may be, so many kinds of voices in the world, and none of them is without signification (1 Corinthians 14:10).

"There are many *kinds* [*genē*—cf. *kinds of tongues*— 1 Corinthians 12:10,28] of *voices* [*phōnōn—sounds*] in the world." In fact, there are more than 3,000 languages on the earth!

Without doubt this verse is speaking of *foreign languages*. The word "voice" is commonly used in the sense of "language." Genesis 11:1 in the Septuagint reads: "And all the earth was one lip, and there was one *language* [lit., voice] to all." In other words, ever since Babel, there have been many kinds of voices in the world! Another example is Deuteronomy 28:49 (Septuagint): "The Lord shall bring upon thee a nation . . . whose *voice* [language] thou shalt not understand." Also in 2 Peter 2:16 the dumb ass spoke in a human *language* that Balaam could understand! So it is

with justification that the NASV translates the verse
as follows: "There are, perhaps, a great many kinds of
languages in the world." And none of these languages
are without signification. They all convey meaning to
those who understand the language. The problem comes
when a person does *not* understand the language!

> Therefore if I know not the meaning of the voice,
> I shall be unto him that speaketh a barbarian, and he that
> speaketh shall be a barbarian unto me (1 Corinthians 14:11).

The problem comes when a person does not know
the meaning of the *voice* (language). This word translated "meaning" (lit., power, force) is used of the significance or force of what is spoken. For example, a
man may preach a *powerful* and *forceful* message, but
if one cannot understand his language, he will not feel
the *impact* of what the preacher is saying, *unless* someone interprets.

A *barbarian* is a foreigner, one who speaks in a
strange, unintelligible tongue.

> If I do not know the meaning of the language [even
> though all languages have meaning—verse 10], I shall be
> a foreigner to the speaker and the speaker a foreigner to
> me" (verse 11 RSV).

Here is verse 11 restated in light of the point Paul
was making: "If I do not know the meaning of the
tongue, I shall be to the tongue-speaker a foreigner, and

the tongue-speaker shall be a foreigner to me"—there would be no communication and thus no edification!

> Even so ye, forasmuch as ye are zealous of spiritual gifts, seek that ye may excel to the edifying of the church. Wherefore let him that speaketh in an unknown tongue pray that he may interpret (1 Corinthians 14:12-13).

God's priority is a healthy assembly, and the Corinthian believers are encouraged to seek that which will edify most of all. Thus, if the gift of tongues is exercised, there *must* be an interpreter! And the tongues-speaker should pray that "one might interpret" (see the previous discussion under verse 5). The *chief concern* of the tongues-speaker is that his message might be interpreted. Otherwise it is of no value to the assembly and he is merely speaking into the air!

> For if I pray in an unknown tongue, my spirit prayeth, but my understanding is unfruitful (1 Corinthians 14:14).

It is possible for a believer to pray in a tongue, but his *understanding* (mind) is unfruitful or fruitless. That is, he does not understand what he is praying. He prays with his spirit but not with his understanding (mind).

> What is it then? I will pray with the spirit, and I will pray with the understanding also: I will sing with the

spirit, and I will sing with the understanding also (1 Corinthians 14:15).

God expects the believer to use his full mental faculties in worship—to worship Him not only in spirit, but in spirit and *in truth* (John 4:23-24; cf. John 4:22, which describes *ignorant worshipers*). The believer must fully concentrate on the *meaning* of what he is praying and what he is singing. Otherwise it can easily become vain repetition. He must *understand* what he is praying and what he is singing.

> Else when thou shalt bless with the spirit, how shall he that occupieth the room of the unlearned say Amen at thy giving of thanks, seeing he understandeth not what thou sayest? For thou verily givest thanks well, but the other is not edified (1 Corinthians 14:16-17).

If a person gives thanks in a tongue, how can anyone say "Amen"? You cannot say "Amen" unless you *understand* what was said and *agree* with what was said.

What was spoken in a tongue was not meaningless utterances or nonsense syllables. In each case Paul makes it clear what the *content* of the tongue was:

Verses 14-15—A prayer to God

Verse 15—A song of praise

Verse 16—The giving of thanks

What was spoken was meaningful, but the meaning was not understood, and "the other was not edified."

> I thank my God, I speak with tongues more than ye all (1 Corinthians 14:18).

Paul himself had the gift of tongues. The problem was not with the gift, but with the *use* of the gift. Paul never implied that the Corinthians did not have the real gift of tongues. Neither did he say that their tongues-speaking was satanic. These believers had a genuine charismatic gift, but it was not being exercised in love. And God was not the author of the confusion that resulted from their fleshly exercise of this gift.

> Yet in the church I had rather speak five words with my understanding, that by my voice I might teach others also, than ten thousand words in an unknown tongue (1 Corinthians 14:19).

What a comparison! Five words that can be understood are better than *ten thousand* words (myriads) in a tongue! Imagine telling a preacher to limit his Sunday morning sermon to five words! (1) Very (2) little (3) can (4) be (5) said! But those five words are better and more edifying than ten thousand words in a tongue!

It takes about one and a half hours to speak ten thousand words! It only takes two seconds to speak five words! Paul would rather take two seconds to say "Christ died for our sins" (1 Corinthians 15:3), than to speak two hours in words not understood. Paul's greatest concern was for the health of the assembly, and he knew that innumerable words in a tongue would all be in vain unless the interpretation was given.

Tongues is here said to consist of *words*. The gift of tongues was not ecstatic utterances; it was words. Tongues-speaking was not nonsense syllables or foolish gibberish; it was *words*! Words must convey meaning. Words are sounds that symbolize and communicate meaning. Trench says that a word (*logos*) is "a word, saying, or *rational* utterance of the mind . . . being as it is the correlative of *reason*."[15] Tongues were not ecstatic utterances; they were rational utterances— *words*! Tongues were such a problem because the words were in a foreign tongue, and therefore not understood (cf. verse 9).

> Brethren, be not children in understanding: howbeit in malice be ye children, but in understanding be men (1 Corinthians 14:20).

Paul now rebukes the Corinthians for their immaturity. They were spiritual babies and they needed to grow up into full manhood and maturity (cf. 1 Corinthians 3:1-2; Ephesians 4:14; Hebrews 5:13). They needed to put away childish things.

CHAPTER 9

THE PURPOSE OF TONGUES
IN THE ASSEMBLY

1 Corinthians 14:21-26

What were tongues for? What was the purpose of this gift? The one place in the New Testament which clearly sets forth the purpose of the gift of tongues is 1 Corinthians 14:22: "Wherefore, *tongues are for* a sign. . . ." The preposition translated "for" (*eis*) here denotes *purpose*. The verse is introduced by the particle "wherefore" (*hōste*), which means "for this reason, therefore."[16] Paul's explanation in verse 22 concerning the purpose of tongues is actually an inference based upon his words in verse 21. Therefore, the key to understanding the purpose of tongues must be found in 1 Corinthians 14:21. Verse 21 begins with these important words, "In the law it is written. . . ."

In verse 21 Paul cited an Old Testament passage, Isaiah 28:11-12. Paul knew that the *key* to understanding the Biblical purpose of tongues is found "in the law," that is, *in the Old Testament Scriptures*. What does

77

the Old Testament teach concerning tongues? What was the significance and purpose of tongues in Old Testament times? When foreign tongues were spoken, what did this mean? The key which will unlock the purpose and significance of the gift of tongues is found "in the law."

Isaiah 28 is not the only passage in the Old Testament which deals with the significance of foreign tongues. Several such passages together set forth a very sobering Biblical principle—a principle which has been demonstrated repeatedly in history. To discover the significance of tongues in the Old Testament, the following important passages must be considered: Genesis 11, Deuteronomy 28, Jeremiah 5, Isaiah 28 (cited by Paul in 1 Corinthians 14:21), and Isaiah 33.

As these passages are examined in detail, the reader is encouraged to discover a pattern and sequence which is repeated again and again. This tragic pattern can be simply summarized as follows:

God has a message for the people.

The people refuse to listen to God.

God causes tongues to be heard as a sign of judgment.

Dispersion follows.

GENESIS 11

In this important chapter describing the judgment upon Babel, *tongues* are mentioned for the very first time. Prior to Genesis 11 tongues (plural) did not exist!

There was only one tongue throughout the inhabited earth: "And the whole earth was of one language, and of one speech" (Genesis 11:1). Foreign tongues made their first historical appearance in Genesis 11.

God has a message for the people. Following the great Genesis flood, God gave this simple command to Noah and his sons: "Be fruitful, and multiply, and fill the earth" (Genesis 9:1; cf. Genesis 9:7). How would the descendants of Noah respond to this divine command?

The people refuse to listen to God. Instead of filling the earth as God had said, the people refused to obey. In their opposition to God's Word and God's will, they decided to build a huge tower and make a name for themselves, "Lest we be scattered abroad over the face of the whole earth" (Genesis 11:4).

God causes tongues to be heard as a sign of judgment. For the first time in history foreign tongues were spoken: "Come, let us go down, and there confound their language, that they may not understand one another's speech" (Genesis 11:7). God's judgment fell upon a disobedient and godless people.

Dispersion followed. "So the Lord scattered them abroad from there upon the face of all the earth" (Genesis 11:8).

DEUTERONOMY 28

The Lord communicated His will to the nation Israel by giving the people His holy law. God set before them a blessing and a curse: a blessing if they would obey the commandments of the Lord, and a curse if they would disobey (Deuteronomy 11:26-28). The blessings and the curses that would come upon the nation are clearly enumerated in Deuteronomy 28.

God has a message for the people.

> And it shall come to pass if thou shalt hearken diligently unto the voice of the LORD thy God, to observe and to do all His commandments which I command thee this day, that the LORD thy God will set thee on high above all nations of the earth; And *all these blessings* shall come on thee, and overtake thee, if thou shalt hearken unto the voice of the LORD thy God" (Deuteronomy 28:1).

The people refuse to listen to God.

> But it shall come to pass, if thou wilt not hearken unto the voice of the LORD thy God, to observe to do all His commandments and His statutes which I command thee this day; that *all these curses* shall come upon thee, and overtake thee (Deuteronomy 28:15).

God causes tongues to be heard as a sign of judgment. One of the curses which the Lord promised to bring upon His disobedient people was the terrible invasion of a conquering nation. As the foreigners would approach, Israel would hear the strange tongues of the enemy:

The LORD shall bring a nation against thee from far, from the end of the earth, as swift as the eagle flieth; *a nation whose tongue thou shalt not understand* (Deuteronomy 28:49).

Dispersion follows.

And the Lord shall scatter thee among all people, from the one end of the earth even unto the other; and there thou shalt serve other gods, which neither thou nor thy fathers have known, even wood and stone. And among these nations shalt thou find no ease, neither shall the sole of thy foot have rest: but the LORD shall give thee there a trembling heart, and failing of eyes, and sorrow of mind (Deuteronomy 28:64-65).

JEREMIAH 5

God has a message for the people. Through the Prophet Jeremiah, the Lord pleaded with His people Israel that they might turn from their evil ways and return to the Lord their God: "If thou wilt return, O Israel, saith the LORD, *return unto Me*" (Jeremiah 4:1; cf. Matthew 11:28). God would have done so much if they had simply turned to Him (Psalm 81:8-16)!

The people refuse to listen to God.

O LORD, are not Thine eyes upon the truth? Thou hast stricken them, but they have not grieved; Thou hast consumed them, but *they have refused to receive correction:* they have made their faces harder than a`rock; *they have refused to return* (Jeremiah 5:3).

God causes tongues to be heard as a sign of judgment. When a people refuse to come to God, judgment must inevitably follow. The forbearance and long-suffering of God must someday come to an end. If Israel would not respond to Jeremiah's warnings, then God would speak to the nation in a way they would never forget. Though they could not understand the strange tongues of their invaders, the message of their swords would be long remembered:

> Lo, I will bring a nation upon you from far, O house of Israel, saith the LORD: it is a mighty nation, it is an ancient nation, *a nation whose language thou knowest not, neither understandest what they say* (Jeremiah 5:15).

Dispersion follows.

> And it shall come to pass, when ye shall say, Wherefore doeth the LORD our God all these things unto us? then shalt thou answer them, Like as ye have forsaken Me, and served strange gods in your land, *so shall ye serve strangers in a land that is not yours* (Jeremiah 5:19).

For Israel, to be in the promised land was a sign of God's blessing. To be out of the land, scattered and persecuted, was a sure indication that they were under God's curse.

ISAIAH 28

In his important discussion concerning the purpose of the gift of tongues (1 Corinthians 14:21-22), the Apostle Paul cites Isaiah 28:11-12 as evidence that tongues was given as a sign "to them that believe not." A proper understanding of this important Old Testament passage is crucial in determining the Biblical purpose of tongues.

In Isaiah 28:9-10 ungodly Jews were apparently mocking the message of God's prophet, Isaiah. They were expressing their indignation at Isaiah's infantile teaching methods! They questioned, "Does he take us grave and revered seigniors, priests, and prophets, to be babies just weaned, that he pesters us with these monotonous petty preachings, fit only for the nursery, which he calls his 'message'?"[1 7]

Isaiah's message was clear and simple and even monotonous! Line upon line, line upon line. . . . Sin brings judgment, sin brings judgment. . . . Turn to God, turn to God. . . . Isaiah used the Chinese water-torture technique of teaching: drop, drop, drop . . . sin, sin, sin . . . judgment, judgment, judgment . . . repent, repent, repent. . . . So it is not a surprise that his hearers began to say, "Who do you think we are, Isaiah? Babies? To whom do you think you are lecturing? Your repetitious preaching is fit for infants: *"Sav lasav sav lasav, kav lakav kav lakav, ze'er sham ze'er sham"* (see NASV marginal note). These unbelieving Jews rejected God's message, they rejected God's messenger, and they rejected God's messenger's teaching methods.

The Lord responded to their unbelieving scoffing by imitating their mockery and setting forth the unintelligible language of a foreign conqueror (verse 11). God first spoke to them through Isaiah's clear and simple message. Now He will speak in *judgment* to them through a foreign tongue. He will speak to them with stammering lips and *another* (different, strange, foreign) tongue (cf. Acts 2:4 and 1 Corinthians 14:21 – "other tongues").

These people closed their ears and refused the proclamation of a heavenly message. God then became, as it were, a barbarian to these people. The Assyrian tongue, which soon surrounded the Israelites, must have sounded to them like the lisping of children. It was a much less cultivated language than Hebrew, and had only the three basic vowels: a, i, and u. Because they would not hear words of comfort in their own language, they had to hear the enemy's harsh sounds.[18]

God graciously would have given the people the *rest* that is found in Himself (cf. Matthew 11:28; Isaiah 30:15-17; Psalm 81:8-16), but they refused to listen. God's wonderful promise of comfort and rest was tragically rejected. The Israelites were sick and tired of Isaiah's repetitive assertions that sin was rampant, judgment was coming, and a return to God was the only answer.

Finally, in verses 11-13 Isaiah tells these mockers that God will indeed speak to this people. This time His message will not come through Isaiah, but through a foreign tongue. When the enemy would enter their borders, killing many, and taking others captive, they would begin to get the message! Once again the terrible pattern is repeated:

God has a message for the people.

> To whom He said, This is the rest wherewith ye may cause the weary to rest; and this is the refreshing (Isaiah 28:12).

The people refuse to listen to God.

> Yet they would not hear (Isaiah 28:12).

God causes tongues to be heard as a sign of judgment.

> For with stammering lips and another tongue will He speak to this people (Isaiah 28:11).

Dispersion follows.

> That they might go, and fall backward, and be broken, and *snared, and taken* (Isaiah 28:13).

ISAIAH 33

To the nation Israel, foreign tongues was a sign of God's judgment and curse upon them. Likewise, the *absence* of foreign tongues is a sign that the nation is under the blessing of God.

In Isaiah 33:17 Israel is given a wonderful promise concerning the future millennial kingdom: "Thine eyes shall see the king in His beauty." Certainly, during the kingdom age, Israel will enjoy God's richest blessings! No longer will they be under God's curse. Never again will they be invaded by foreign nations. They will dwell safely and securely in the land of promise, protected by the King Himself. Thus, the absence of foreign tongues will be a sign of God's abundant blessing upon the nation:

> You will no longer see a fierce people, a people of unintelligible speech which no one comprehends, of a stammering tongue which no one understands" (Isaiah 33:19 NASV).

THE PATTERN REPEATED
IN THE NEW TESTAMENT

Those who fail to learn from the lessons of history are bound to repeat its mistakes. The Assyrian and Babylonian captivities should have taught Israel a lesson. On the pages of the New Testament, however, the same disastrous pattern emerges.

God has a message for the people.

> Come unto Me . . . and I will give you rest (Matthew 11:28; cf. Jeremiah 4:1; Isaiah 28:12).

The people refuse to listen to God.

> O Jerusalem, Jerusalem, thou that killest the prophets, and stonest them which are sent unto thee, how often would I have gathered thy children together, even as a hen gathereth her chickens under her wings, and *ye would not* [you were not willing, you refused] (Matthew 23:37).

God causes tongues to be heard as a sign of judgment. The Lord Jesus predicted the terrible judgment that would come upon the nation which had refused God and rejected His Messiah:

> Behold, your house is left unto you desolate. . . . Verily I say unto you, There shall not be left here one stone upon another, that shall not be thrown down (Matthew 23:38; 24:2).

The destruction of Jerusalem took place in 70 A.D. as the city was invaded by the Roman armies, led by General Titus. For the next two thousand years the living God would not dwell in a temple made with hands, but He would dwell in a unique body of believers, and in each member in particular (1 Corinthians 3:16-17; 1 Corinthians 6:19). God's program was shifting from Israel to the Church.

Years earlier God had caused foreign tongues to be spoken and heard as a judgmental sign to the nation Israel (Acts 2; 10; 19, etc.). For those Jews who were familiar with their Old Testament, the sounds of foreign tongues gave no cause for rejoicing! Tongues were a sign of God's curse, not of God's blessing. Tongues signified a coming invasion, and conveyed an ominous message of rebellion, judgment, and dispersion. When God spoke in tongues, the Jews understood the message (Isaiah 28:11; 1 Corinthians 14:21). Tongues were a sign-gift, given to an unbelieving, Christ-rejecting nation:

> "Wherefore tongues are for a sign, not to them that believe, but to them that believe not" (1 Corinthians 14:22).

Dispersion follows. The nation Israel has been scattered throughout the world for nearly two thousand years! They have been out of the land, severely persecuted, and God's curse has been upon them: *"His blood be on us, and on our children"* (Matthew 27:25). Although a small remnant has returned to the land, the nation is still without a temple and there is no rest or peace in the land. The destruction of Jerusalem by Titus in 70 A.D. was something from which the nation of Israel has never recovered!

THE DURATION OF TONGUES

When did tongues cease? If foreign tongues were really a *sign of coming judgment* upon the nation Israel, then once this judgment had come, the sign-gift would no longer be necessary. Any Jew who knew his Old Testament should have recognized foreign tongues as a solemn warning of coming judgment. Once the judgment had come, the warning sign was no longer needed!

God graciously waited four decades following the crucifixion of His Son (Israel's rejected Messiah) before He brought final judgment upon the nation. But in 70 A.D. the Romans under General Titus brought the Christ-rejecting nation to its final ruin. Ever since A.D. 70 there has been no question that Israel as a nation is under the judgment of God. The Jews have been forced out of the land. They have been scattered and persecuted throughout the world. It is obvious that God is no longer working through His chosen *nation*. His program has now shifted and God's witnesses are among all *nations*. The Jews are *out of the land*, a definite sign that they are now under God's curse (cf. Deuteronomy 28).

In every nation where they have been scattered they constantly hear foreign tongues (Russian, German, English, etc.) as a continual reminder to them that they have refused the blessing and rest of God. Interestingly enough, not one book in the New Testament was written in the language of the Jews. Not only did God shift from Israel to the Church, but He also shifted from Hebrew to Greek as the language through which He would give His Word! God has not cast away His people Israel (Romans 11:1), but He has cast them aside for a time. The final and ultimate event which marked Israel's judgment was the destruction of Jerusalem in 70 A.D., an event that was predicted by our Lord forty years before (Matthew 23:38; 24:2).

Therefore, it must be concluded that tongues as a

sign-gift were no longer needed after 70 A.D. *Tongues must have ceased on or before 70 A.D.* The last historical mention of the gift of tongues is in 1 Corinthians which was written about 55 A.D. There is no evidence historically that the genuine gift of tongues ever occurred after 70 A.D. Tongues served their purpose, and *tongues ceased*, even as God had predicted through the Apostle Paul (1 Corinthians 13:8).

> Wherefore tongues are for a sign, not to them that believe, but to them that believe not: but prophesying serveth not for them that believe not, but for them which believe (1 Corinthians 14:22).

As previously noted, tongues were a *sign* for the unbelieving, rebellious, Christ-rejecting nation of Israel. The *believers* in the Corinthian assembly needed to understand the purpose of tongues, but much more they needed to avail themselves of the gift of prophecy, which is valuable towards edification and exhortation and comfort (verse 3). Not only is prophecy of value for believers, but prophecy is also of value for potential believers (those visiting the assembly), as Paul explains in verses 23-25.

It is important to realize that the unbelievers mentioned in 1 Corinthians 14:21-22 are very different than the unbelievers mentioned in 1 Corinthians 14:23-24, even though the same Greek word is used (*apistos*). In verses 21-22 Paul describes rebellious and disobedient unbelievers, who heard God's message but then refused it and even rejected the God who gave it. These were unbelievers who would not hear God (1 Corinthians 14:21). They stubbornly refused God's gracious offer of rest (Isaiah 28:12). These were unbelievers who belonged to "this people" (1 Corinthians 14:21; Isaiah 28:11), which in the context of the Isaiah passage can refer only to the people of Israel, the Jews. Tongues were a foreboding sign of coming judgment for an unbelieving nation who would not listen to their God.

But the unbelievers described in 1 Corinthians 14:23-24 are in marked contrast to the rebellious, God-rejecting Jews just mentioned. These were unbelievers who had come into the assembly. Paul was most likely thinking of unbelieving Gentiles who decided they would visit the Corinthian church and see what was going on there. They were willing to come and to listen to whatever the church had to offer. Apparently these unbelievers were seekers. In fact, they were *potential believers!* Paul knew that the one thing potential believers need more than anything else is prophecy, not tongues.

The Bible teaches, in 1 Corinthians 14:22, that tongues served as a judgmental sign to the nation Israel.[19] Does this mean that wherever tongues were spoken, there had to be unbelieving Jews present? Such a position is very problematic. Why would a rebellious, Christ-rejecting Jew be present at a church service in Corinth? Assembling with Christians would be the last thing he would want to do. Also, there were no unbelieving Jews present in Acts 10 or Acts 19, when the tongues-speaking occurred. The Bible never says that unbelieving

Jews must be present whenever tongues are spoken, and
Paul did not include this in his list of regulations in
1 Corinthians 14:27-35.

But then could tongues serve as a sign to the Jews?
It should be understood that the unbelieving Jews in
the Roman empire knew about the Christian church.
They were conscious of the Christian community in their
midst. The Christians were the talk of the synagogue!
Indeed, the Jews were very much aware of the fact that
some of these Christians had the amazing ability to speak
in foreign languages—languages that they had never
learned. They had at least heard of this amazing phenomenon.

How can it be said that the unbelieving Jews were
aware of the gift of tongues? It is important to think
back to the day in which the Church first began and
tongues were first heard. On the day of Pentecost there
were assembled Jews "from every nation under heaven"
(Acts 2:5-6). These Jews all witnessed the gift of tongues
in operation. Many of them believed the gospel as Peter
preached it, but many did not (compare the "mockers"
of Acts 2:13). As these Jews returned to their homes
they must have told their kinsmen about the remarkable
things which they saw and heard. One can almost
imagine such a conversation:

"Have you heard what went on at Jerusalem? The
followers of Jesus of Nazareth were claiming that their
leader had come back from the dead. On the day of
Pentecost the most amazing thing happened! They spoke
in foreign languages. It was remarkable! The men who

spoke in these tongues were Galileans!"

Many years go by and then: "Do you remember when you told me about that tongues-speaking in Jerusalem? Well, certain Christians have started meeting in our city and I have heard a report that some of them speak in foreign languages also!"

It is not necessary to be present in a church to know what takes place there. Reports go out and word gets around! In the days of the early Church people were aware, at least to some degree, of what was taking place in the Christian assemblies. The same was true in Old Testament times. When the Assyrians or Babylonians came to invade the land, the news was spread quickly. The Jews did not need to see their enemies and hear them speak to know that they were coming!

In 1 Corinthians 14:22, the Greek article precedes the word "tongues" in verse 22 and is very significant. It is an article of previous reference (pointing back to what has just been mentioned).

"Wherefore *the* tongues are for a sign."

"What tongues are you talking about, Paul?"

"The tongues I just finished talking about in verse 21, namely foreign tongues."

Thus if the tongues in verse 21 are foreign languages (Isaiah 28), then the tongues in verse 22 (the Corinthian tongues) must be the same thing.

> If therefore the whole church be come together into one place, and all speak with tongues, and there come in those that are unlearned, or unbelievers, will they not say

that ye are mad? But if all prophesy, and there come in one that believeth not, or one unlearned, he is convinced of all, he is judged of all: And thus are the secrets of his heart made manifest; and so falling down on his face he will worship God, and report that God is in you of a truth (1 Corinthians 14:23-25).

In order for the Corinthian assembly to have an effective testimony before the lost, its members must manifest the life of Christ. The world needs to see a healthy, growing *organism* (not organization). The number one characteristic of an organism is that it possesses life. The local church is animated by the very life of God (cf. 1 Timothy 3:15—"the assembly of the *living God*"). The assembly is pulsating with God's life because it is indwelt by the living Christ (Colossians 1:27).

During our Lord's incarnate life and ministry here upon the earth, *God was manifested in the flesh!* But the great mystery that thrilled the heart of the Apostle Paul is that *today* God is incarnate in a body upon this earth (1 Timothy 3:15-16; Colossians 1:26-27). Christ now has a body on the earth, in addition to His resurrected body in Heaven.

The world cannot see Christ directly, because He is in Heaven, but it can see His body which is upon the earth—a living organism manifesting the heavenly, resurrected life of Christ! The Head is in Heaven, but the body is upon the earth, for the purpose of bearing witness to the Head! And there is only one way that the world can see Christ today. It must see *"Christ in you!"* (Colossians 1:27) It must see Christ in the Church, because Christ is today manifesting Himself in a body, which is His Church, "the fulness of Him that filleth all in all" (Ephesians 1:23). How precious the assembly must be to the Lord!

According to Colossians 1:27-28, there is only one way that the living Christ can truly manifest Himself in and through the assembly. *Every* single member of the body must be warned, *every* single body member must be taught, and *every* single member of the body must be well fed! When the members are well fed, then the body is going to be healthy; when the body is healthy, then the life of Christ will be manifested, sinners will be convicted, and God will be glorified!

In 1 Timothy 3:15 Paul describes the local Church as the house of God, indicating that the Most High God lives and dwells in the assembly. What a marvel— the indwelling presence of the living God in the Church! If the expression, "house of God" (*oikos theou*) were to be translated into Hebrew, the resultant word would be *Bethel* (*Beyt-el*). If one is ever going to understand the New Testament "Bethel" (1 Timothy 3:15), then he must first realize what Jacob discovered about the Old Testament Bethel in Genesis 28.

When Jacob awoke from his dream, he exclaimed, "Surely *the LORD is in this place;* and I knew it not. And he was afraid, and said, How dreadful is this place! *this is none other but the house of God....* And he called the name of that place *Bethel*" (Genesis 28:16-19).

"The LORD is in this place" and Jacob did not even realize it! And those who belong to the New Testament Bethel often fail to realize this very thing. Paul wrote to the Corinthian "Bethel" and said, "Know ye not that ye are the temple of God, and that the Spirit of God dwelleth in you?" (1 Corinthians 3:16) God dwells in the assembly. The Church is the habitation of God through the Spirit (Ephesians 2:22).

Ephesians 4:11-16 makes it very clear that God's priority is a healthy organism. In 1 Corinthians 14 (especially verses 3,4,5,12,17) it has been noted that the body of believers must be edified and healthy. The world needs to see a healthy assembly, not a sick one!

What will happen when an unsaved person comes into an assembly that is functioning *contrary* to the principles of edification? The answer is found in 1 Corinthians 14:23. He will say, "This is a madhouse! These people are out of their minds!" But what a difference when he comes into an assembly that is functioning according to principles of edification (verses 24-25). Now he sees a healthy organism, and he sees Christlike saints! So, falling down on his face he will worship God and say, "God is in these people. God is in this place. How dreadful is this place. This is none other than the house of God. This is not a madhouse. This is the house of God! Bethel."

Is this what unbelievers notice as they come into local churches today? Do they see a healthy organism? Do they see well-fed members? Do they see "Christ in you"? Are they convicted by the awesome Presence and Person of God?

The greatest testimony before the world results when the local church functions as an "edificational center," not as an "evangelistic center." The greatest need today is for a lost world to see the Lord Jesus Christ manifesting Himself in and through a healthy assembly of believers. This cannot be produced by preaching "John 3:16" salvation sermons every Sunday. The saints need nothing less than a steady diet of the whole counsel of God (Acts 20:26-32; Matthew 28:20; 2 Timothy 4:1-2; etc.).

> How is it then, brethren? when ye come together, every one of you hath a psalm, hath a doctrine, hath a tongue, hath a revelation, hath an interpretation. Let all things be done unto edifying (1 Corinthians 14:26).

Paul now gives the summarization of the last twenty-five verses. *"Let all things be done unto edifying."* In contrast, the motto of many "soul-winning" churches today seems to be,"Let all things be done unto evangelism." But the Apostle Paul realized that a lost and dying world needs to see Christlike believers who understand and practice God's Word. When God's people are fully equipped for the work of the ministry (Ephesian 4:11-16), they certainly will not be lax in gospel outreach, nor allow mission programs to suffer. When a church makes its priority that of edification, then true evangelism cannot help but be enhanced, as 1 Corinthians 14:24-25 illustrates so well.

Interestingly enough, the cults do not establish evangelistic centers. Rather they establish edificational centers to train their people to go out and do the work of the ministry. The people are immersed in a program of total indoctrination. The average Jehovah's Witness, for example, is ready always to give an answer to every man that asks him a reason of the false hope that is within him. The average Bible believer is horribly ignorant of God's truth. The devil knows what system really works! The cults do not lack for converts.

CHAPTER 10

THE REGULATION OF TONGUES IN THE ASSEMBLY

1 Corinthians 14:27-40

Paul, in correcting the misuse of tongues in Corinth, set forth certain regulations for the proper use of tongues in the assembly. The governing principles behind all of these regulations are summed up in verse 26 ("Let all things be done unto edifying") and in verse 40 ("Let all things be done decently and in order"). Paul did not forbid the Corinthians to speak with tongues (verse 39) but he did forbid any tongues-speaking contrary to the rules which he set forth.

> If any man speak in an unknown tongue, let it be by two, or at the most by three, and that by course; and let one interpret (1 Corinthians 14:27).

Regulation 1—No more than three people could speak in tongues on any one occasion.

Regulation 2—The tongues-speakers must speak

one after another in succession, not all at once.

In other words, they were to speak one at a time (each in turn) and not over three in all were to speak.

Regulation 3—Whenever tongues-speaking occurs, there must also be the interpretation of the tongues.

> But if there be no interpreter, let him keep silence in the church; and let him speak to himself, and to God (1 Corinthians 14:28).

Regulation 4—If there is no interpreter, then the tongues-speaker must keep silent.

This verse indicates that the gift of tongues was something that could be controlled by the speaker. It was in his power to shut it off! If tongues were misused, he was responsible. The spirits of the tongues-speakers were subject to the tongues-speakers.

> Let the prophets speak two or three, and let the other judge. If any thing be revealed to another that sitteth by, let the first hold his peace. For ye may all prophesy one by one, that all may learn, and all may be comforted (1 Corinthians 14:29-31).

Paul now gives some regulations for those who were gifted as prophets. There was a great need for spiritual discernment when the prophets spoke, lest a false prophet should be found in their midst (cf. 1 Corinthians 12:10—the gift of "discerning of spirits"). Also there were to be no private sessions (verses 30-31).

Let all profit from the prophet!

> And the spirits of the prophets are subject to the prophets. For God is not the author of confusion, but of peace, as in all the churches of the saints (1 Corinthians 14:32-33).

The exercise of the gift of prophecy was not something out of the prophet's control. The prophet could never say, "I could not help it! The Holy Spirit came upon me and I just had to speak!" No, the spirits of the prophets were subject to the prophets. The person who exercised the gift of prophecy was not overwhelmed by some external force which carried him beyond his control. On the contrary, he was able to speak or wait his turn or refrain from speaking. He knew what he was doing and he was accountable for his actions. The gifted man was responsible for how he used the gift.

Unger has explained verse 32 as follows: "The prophet (or the speaker in tongues) when exercising his gift is not under an irresistible compulsion or force, so that he is unable to conform to common sense regulations and orderly conduct."[20]

If the prophecy were to get out of control, then the prophet would be blamed, "for God is not the author of confusion" (verse 33). God must not be blamed for the Corinthian problem. The Corinthians themselves were responsible for the confusion in their assembly.

Not even the devil could be blamed for the disorder and confusion in Corinth. In these chapters, Paul never suggested that the Corinthian tongues-speaking was of the devil, though certainly Satan was pleased by the havoc produced in this carnal assembly.

The gift of tongues, even at Corinth, was a God-given gift. God enabled some of the Corinthian believers to speak in a language they had never learned. Paul never implied that the gift was illegitimate or spurious. He never said that the Corinthians did not have the real gift of tongues. In fact, if the gift of tongues at Corinth were not genuine, then it is unthinkable that Paul would have said, "forbid not to speak with tongues" (verse 39; cf. verses 5,18).

Though the gift was legitimate, Paul taught that it was the least edifying of all the gifts (1 Corinthians 12:28), and of little value compared to the gift of prophecy (1 Corinthians 14:2-3). Paul declared that tongues were of no edificational value, unless there was interpretation (1 Corinthians 14:27-28).

The problem was not with the gift. The problem was that the Corinthians were abusing and misusing the gift God had given them. They failed to exercise the gift of tongues in a decent and orderly way (1 Corinthians 14:40). The confusion came because the carnal Corinthians were operating not according to love, but according to the flesh (cf. James 3:16 and 1 Corinthians 3:3-4).

> Let your women keep silence in the churches: for it is not permitted unto them to speak; but they are commanded to be under obedience, as also saith the law. And if they will learn any thing, let them ask their husbands

at home: for it is a shame for women to speak in the church (1 Corinthians 14:34-35).

Regulation 5—The women were not to speak in tongues in the assembly.

What? came the word of God out from you? or came it unto you only? If any man think himself to be a prophet, or spiritual, let him acknowledge that the things that I write unto you are the commandments of the Lord. But if any man be ignorant, let him be ignorant (1 Corinthians 14:36-38).

These regulations were to be heeded and obeyed as if Christ Himself had given them. In fact, Christ did give them! These are the commandments of the Lord. Beware lest some have a "red-letter edition" understanding of the New Testament. The entire New Testament should be in *red* (cf. John 16:12) and should be *read* as authoritative (2 Timothy 3:16).

Wherefore, brethren, covet to prophesy, and forbid not to speak with tongues (1 Corinthians 14:39).

Notice the superior edificational value of prophecy:
Verse 1—"But much more desire that ye may prophesy"
Verse 5—"But much more I desire that ye prophesied"
Verse 22—"Prophecy is for those who believe"
Verse 39—"Covet [zealously seek] to prophesy"
On the other hand, Paul did not forbid tongues-

speaking. Tongues had a God-given purpose and place as a sign-gift (verse 22).

The command, "forbid not to speak with tongues," was written about 55 A.D.—*before* tongues had ceased. When tongues ceased, then the command was no longer in effect. How can a gift be exercised when the gift is no longer given? If tongues were no longer needed after 70 A.D. (as discussed in chapter 9), then since 70 A.D. no one has had the God-given charismatic gift of tongues. So the command, "forbid not to speak with tongues," no longer applies today. One cannot forbid a person to do something that is no longer done! That would be like a person today forbidding a prophet to speak (cf. 1 Thessalonians 5:20). Can someone forbid a prophet to speak when there are no longer any prophets? But in Paul's day (55 A.D.) the gift of tongues was still in effect and was to be regulated, but was not to be forbidden or hindered.[21]

> Let all things be done decently and in order (1 Corinthians 14:40).

This verse implies that the Corinthians were doing things indecently and out of order! God's people must know how to conduct themselves in the house of God, which is the church of the living God, the pillar and base of the truth (1 Timothy 3:15). Only then will the living God manifest His glorious Person and Presence in and through the assembly (1 Timothy 3:16).

APPENDIX 1

TWELVE REASONS WHY
BIBLICAL TONGUES
WERE REAL LANGUAGES

TWELVE REASONS WHY BIBLICAL TONGUES WERE REAL LANGUAGES

1. The term "tongue" is often used in the New Testament describing real languages (Revelation 5:9; 7:9; 10:11; 11:9; 13:7; 14:6; 17:15).

2. The adjective "new" is most appropriate for describing real languages (Mark 16:17).

    Tongues were the God-given ability to speak in a language that was totally new to the speaker (i.e., a foreign language). How could ecstatic utterances be thought of as being "new"?

3. Speaking in tongues was a supernatural, God-given ability (Mark 16:17-18; Acts 2:4) which is reasonable only if tongues were real languages.

    As John Walvoord observes, "Any view which denies that speaking in tongues used actual languages is difficult to harmonize with the scriptural concept of a spiritual gift. By its nature, a spiritual gift had reality, and being supernatural, needs no naturalistic explanation."[22]

Bellshaw adds this comment: "If these tongues are ecstatic utterances, they could be duplicated fraudulently. Gibberish can be uttered by anyone, and a second person could feign interpretation of that unintelligible vocalization. Therefore, it is reasonable that this gift would consist of the ability to speak in a foreign language without the opportunity to learn that language by ordinary means."[23]

4. The adjective "other" is most appropriate for describing real languages (Acts 2:4; 1 Corinthians 14:21; Isaiah 28:11).

These are languages *other* than and *different* from the person's native tongue (i.e., foreign languages). In what sense could ecstatic utterances be considered "different"?

5. The tongues of Acts 2:4,11 are clearly identified in Acts 2:6,8 as real languages (dialects).

6. The tongues in the book of Acts were not meaningless utterances, but they were means of conveying a meaningful message (Acts 2:11; 10:46). Likewise the tongues in 1 Corinthians communicated meaningful content.

In Acts:

Acts 2:4—"the great things of God"

Acts 10:46—"magnifying God (proclaiming God's greatness)"

Thus, tongues in Acts involved meaningful doctrinal content, not meaningless and empty gibberish.

In 1 Corinthians:

1 Corinthians 14:14-15—A prayer to God

1 Corinthians 14:15—A song of praise

1 Corinthians 14:16—The giving of thanks

7. The expression "kinds of tongues" is understandable only if tongues were real languages (1 Corinthians 12:10,28; cf. 1 Corinthians 14:10).

Any linguist knows that the three thousand languages of the world are *grouped* into many classes or kinds. But could it be said that there are *kinds of ecstatic utterances?*

8. The fact that tongues could be *interpreted* demands that tongues be real languages (1 Corinthians 12:10,30; 14:5,13,27-28).

Interpretation necessitates meaning! Meaningless utterances cannot be interpreted. How can one give meaning to something that has no meaning? How can one give sense to nonsense?

9. 1 Corinthians 14:10-11 is clearly depicting real languages.

10. Tongues-speaking is said to consist of *words*, which would be possible only if tongues were real languages (1 Corinthians 14:9,19).

11. The tongues mentioned in Isaiah 28:11 (cited by Paul in 1 Corinthians 14:21) were real languages.

12. The article of previous reference in 1 Corinthians 14:22 proves that the Corinthian tongues (verse 22) were the very same thing as the Isaiah tongues (verse 21), namely, real languages (see discussion, page 93).

CONCLUSION

"These twelve arguments, taken together, demonstrate conclusively that all of the New Testament references to the gift of tongues concern the same phenomenon. In every case it was the miraculous ability to speak in an unlearned foreign language."[24]

APPENDIX 2

1 CORINTHIANS 13:8 AND
TEMPORARY GIFTS

1 CORINTHIANS 13:8 AND TEMPORARY GIFTS

The spiritual gifts listed by Paul in 1 Corinthians 12:8-11 are grouped into three categories (see page 50):

Category 1

the word of wisdom
the word of *knowledge*

Category 2

faith
gifts of healing
working of miracles
prophecy
discerning of spirits

Category 3

kinds of *tongues*
interpretation of tongues

In the very next chapter, three of these gifts are mentioned again as Paul discusses the permanence of love:

> Love never fails; but if there are gifts of *prophecy*, they will be done away; if there are *tongues*, they will cease; if there is *knowledge*, it will be done away (1 Corinthians 13:8, NASV).

From each category, Paul selected one gift. Is it possible that Paul intended the one gift to represent the entire category? Often in Scripture, the part is put for the whole, a figure of speech called "synecdoche." Instead of laboriously listing all the gifts, which he had just done in the previous chapter, Paul could have easily listed one representative gift to stand for each of the three categories.

If this interpretation is correct, then what Paul says about each gift would be true for all of the gifts in the category. For example, if tongues were to cease, then obviously the gift of interpretation would necessarily cease as well. Once tongues had ceased, there would no longer be a need for interpretation. Thus, according to 1 Corinthians 13:8, the gifts in categories 1 and 2 would be *done away* (rendered inoperative), and the gifts in category 3 would cease. All of the gifts listed in 1 Corinthians 12:8-11, therefore, should be considered as temporary gifts.

The gifts of knowledge and wisdom were special revelatory gifts which were needed in the days prior to the completed New Testament (cf. 1 Corinthians 13:2). Imagine a local church today trying to survive without the New Testament Scriptures as a pattern and guide! Divine knowledge and wisdom were essential in the infancy period of the early Church. Today, "all truth" which is necessary for the godly walk of believers has been recorded on the pages of the completed Bible (cf. John 16:13).

The second category contains several individual gifts—faith, healing, miracles, prophecy, and discerning of spirits. Certainly, as prophecy was done away (1 Corinthians 13:8), there no longer would be a need for discerning of spirits. If there were no more true prophets, then it would not take much discernment to spot a false one!

The temporary character of the miraculous gifts (gifts of healing and miracles) is explained in Hebrews 2:3-4:

> How shall we escape, if we neglect so great salvation, which at the first began to be spoken by the Lord, and was confirmed unto us by them that heard Him, God also bearing them witness, both with signs and wonders, and with diverse miracles and gifts of the Holy Spirit, according to His own will?

These sign-gifts were given to authenticate and confirm the word of the apostles (cf. Mark 16:17,20).

Most commentators agree that the gift of faith was a special "miracle-working" or "wonder-working" faith (cf. 1 Corinthians 13:2; Matthew 17:19-20; 21:21). The gift of faith, possessed by only some believers, should not be confused with faith as a Christian virtue (1 Corinthians 13:13) possessed by every believer. "Miracle-working" faith is best illustrated by the healing of the lame man in Acts 3:

> And His name through *faith* in His name hath made this man strong, whom ye see and know: yea, the *faith* which is by Him hath given him this perfect soundness in the presence of you all (Acts 3:16; cf. Acts 6:8).

Peter was given a special gift of faith in order to trust Christ for this remarkable miracle!

When the gifts of healing and miracles were terminated, there was no longer a need for the special gift of "miracle-working" faith. Thus, all gifts in category 2 were most likely done away before the end of the first century.

As this study has suggested, the gifts of knowledge, tongues, and prophecy (1 Corinthians 13:8) are representative of all three categories of gifts. If this is true, then it follows that all nine of the gifts listed in 1 Corinthians 12:8-11 were temporary gifts and ceased or were done away in the apostolic period.

REFERENCES

REFERENCES

Most Bible references in this paper were taken from the King James Version of the Bible. Other versions were used where it would help elucidate the meaning of the Greek text. The use of a translation does not mean that the writer endorses the translation as a whole. The following abbreviations have been used:

KJV (Authorized King James Version, 1611)
RV (Revised Version, 1881)
RSV (Revised Standard Version, 1952)
NASV (New American Standard Version, 1960)

[1] William F. Arndt and F. Wilbur Gingrich, *A Greek-English Lexicon of the New Testament and Other Early Christian Literature* (Chicago: The University of Chicago Press, 1957), pp. 394-395.

[2] Merrill F. Unger, *New Testament Teaching on Tongues* (Grand Rapids: Kregel Publications, 1971), p. 34.

[3] C. Norman Sellers, *Biblical Conclusions Concerning Tongues* (Miami: C.N. Sellers, 1972), p. 6 (footnote).

119

4 Robert G. Gromacki, *The Modern Tongues Movement* (Nutley, New Jersey: Presbyterian and Reformed Publishing Company, 1972), p. 60.

5 Joseph Henry Thayer, *Thayer's Greek-English Lexicon of the New Testament* (Grand Rapids: Associated Publishers and Authors Inc., n.d.), p. 147.

6 James L. Boyer, *For a World Like Ours—Studies in 1 Corinthians* (Winona Lake, Indiana: BMH Books, 1971), p. 134.

7 Robert Thomas, "Tongues . . . Will Cease," *Journal of the Evangelical Theological Society,* Vol. 17, No. 2, Spring 1974, pp. 81-89.

8 Joseph Dillow, *Speaking in Tongues—Seven Crucial Questions* (Grand Rapids: Zondervan, 1975), pp. 119-133. Dillow devotes 76 pages to answer the question, "Did the gift of tongues pass from the Church?" (pp. 88-164)

9 Richard Quebedeaux, *The New Charismatics— The Origins, Development, and Significance of Neo-Pentecostalism* (Garden City, New York: Doubleday, 1976), pp. 20-21.

10 Charles R. Smith, *Tongues in Biblical Perspective* (Winona Lake, Indiana: BMH Books, 1972), p. 91.

11 *Ibid.*, pp. 87-92.

12 Sellers, pp. 18-19.

13 John C. Whitcomb, Jr., *Does God Want Christians To Perform Miracles Today?* (Winona Lake, Indiana: BMH Books, 1973), pp. 13-16.

14 Dillow, pp. 147-164.

15 Richard Chenevix Trench, *Synonyms of the*

New Testament (Grand Rapids: Associated Publishers and Authors Inc., n.d.), p. 312.

[16]Arndt and Gingrich, p. 908.

[17]Alexander Maclaren, *The Book of Isaiah: Chapters 1-48* (6th ed.; London: Hodder and Stoughton, n.d.), p. 478.

[18] John Peter Lange, *Commentary on the Holy Scriptures: Isaiah,* trans. and ed. by Philip Schaff (Grand Rapids: Zondervan, n.d.), p. 306.

[19]George E. Gardiner, *The Corinthian Catastrophe* (Grand Rapids: Kregel, 1974), pp. 35-36. See also the excellent discussion by Dillow, pp. 26-34.

[20]Unger, pp. 123-124.

[21]See Dillow, pp. 165-172.

[22]John F. Walvoord, *The Holy Spirit* (Grand Rapids: Zondervan, 1958), p. 182.

[23]William G. Bellshaw, "The Confusion of Tongues," *Bibliotheca Sacra*, Vol. 120 (April-June, 1963), pp. 147-148.

[24]This is Seller's conclusion, p. 7. On pages 1-7 Sellers gives 13 reasons showing that Biblical tongues were real languages. See also Robert H. Gundry, "Ecstatic Utterance (N.E.B.)?" *Journal of Theological Studies*, Vol. 17, 1966, pp. 299-307. Dr. Gundry shows that the tongues speech of both Acts 2 and 1 Corinthians 12–14 can refer only to known languages spoken here on earth.

BIBLIOGRAPHY

BIBLIOGRAPHY

Arndt, William G., and Gingrich, R. Wilbur. *A Greek-English Lexicon of the New Testament and Other Early Christian Literature.* Chicago: The University of Chicago Press, 1957; Grand Rapids, Zondervan.

Bellshaw, William G. "The Confusion of Tongues." *Bibliotheca Sacra*, Vol. 120 (April-June), 1963.

Boyer, James L. *For a World Like Ours—Studies in 1 Corinthians.* Winona Lake, Indiana: BMH Books, 1971; Grand Rapids, Baker.

Dillow, Jody. *Speaking in Tongues.* Grand Rapids: Zondervan, 1975.

Gardiner, George E. *The Corinthian Catastrophe.* Grand Rapids: Kregel, 1974.

Gromacki, Robert G. *The Modern Tongues Movement.* Nutley, New Jersey: Presbyterian and Reformed Publishing Company, 1972.

Gundry, Robert. "Ecstatic Utterance (N.E.B.)?" *Journal of Theological Studies,* Vol. 17, 1966, 299-307.

Lange, John Peter. *Commentary on the Holy Scriptures: Isaiah.* Translated and edited by Philip Schaff. Grand Rapids: Zondervan, n.d.

125

Maclaren, Alexander. *The Book of Isaiah: Chapters 1–48*. 6th edition. London: Hodder and Stoughton, n.d.

Quebedeaux, Richard. *The New Charismatics—The Origins, Development, and Significance of Neo-Pentecostalism*. Garden City, New York: Doubleday, 1976.

Sellers, C. Norman. *Biblical Conclusions Concerning Tongues*. Miami: C.N. Sellers, 1972.

Smith, Charles R. *Tongues in Biblical Perspective*. Winona Lake, Indiana: BMH Books, 1972.

Thayer, Joseph Henry. *Thayer's Greek-English Lexicon of the New Testament*. Grand Rapids: Associated Publishers and Authors, Inc., n.d.

Thomas, Robert. "Tongues . . . Will Cease," *Journal of the Evangelical Theological Society*, Vol. 17, No. 2, Spring 1974, 81-89.

Trench, Richard Chenevix. *Synonyms of the New Testament*. Grand Rapids: Eerdmans, 1950.

Unger, Merrill F. *New Testament Teaching On Tongues*. Grand Rapids: Kregel, 1971.

Walvoord, John F. *The Holy Spirit*. Grand Rapids: Zondervan, 1958.

Whitcomb, John C. *Does God Want Christians To Perform Miracles Today?* Winona Lake, Indiana: BMH Books, 1973.